Folklore of the New Jersey Shore

Ghosts • the Supernatural • and Beyond

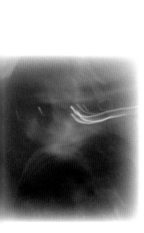

4880 Lower Valley Road • Atglen, PA 19310

Richard J. Kimmel

&

Karen E. Timper

Cover photo by Karen Timper

Published by Schiffer Publishing, Ltd.
4880 Lower Valley Road
Atglen, PA 19310
Phone: (610) 593-1777; Fax: (610) 593-2002
E-mail: Info@schifferbooks.com

For the largest selection of fine reference books on this and related subjects,
please visit our website at:
www.schifferbooks.com.
You may also write for a free catalog.

This book may be purchased from the publisher.
Please try your bookstore first.

We are always looking for people to write books on new and related subjects.
If you have an idea for a book, please contact us at
proposals@schifferbooks.com

Schiffer Books are available at special discounts for bulk purchases for sales promotions or premiums.
Special editions, including personalized covers, corporate imprints, and excerpts can be created in large
quantities for special needs. For more information contact the publisher.

In Europe, Schiffer books are distributed by
Bushwood Books
6 Marksbury Ave.
Kew Gardens
Surrey TW9 4JF England
Phone: 44 (0) 20 8392 8585; Fax: 44 (0) 20 8392 9876
E-mail: info@bushwoodbooks.co.uk
Website: www.bushwoodbooks.co.uk

Other Schiffer Books by the Author:
Ghosts of Central New Jersey: Bizarre, Strange, & Deadly, 978-0-7643-3442-9, $14.99
WW II Ghosts: Artifacts Can Talk, 978-0-7643-3159-6, $14.99

Other Schiffer Books on Related Subjects:
New Jersey Haunts, 978-0-7643-3532-7, $14.99
Cape May Haunts: Elaine's Haunted Mansion and Other Eerie Beach Tales, 978-0-7643-2821-3, $14.95

Copyright © 2012 by Richard J. Kimmel & Karen E. Timper
Unless otherwise noted, images are the property of the authors.
Library of Congress Control Number: 2012941290

Designed by Mark David Bowyer
Type set in Haunt AOE / NewBaskerville BT

ISBN: 978-0-7643-4127-4
Printed in China

Contents

Dedication

James A. Michael
1938 – 2010

Jim and his wife Alice joined New Jersey Ghost Organization two years after we founded the group. Jim had already retired and he and Alice were believers in the paranormal. Jim came ready to explore and always had his camera on many investigations. What we enjoyed the most were the times Jim and Alice returned from a vacation and always shared their photos, which always seemed to have had paranormal activity in them. Both Jim and Alice were very supportive of the group's accomplishments and very proud to be members. Most importantly, Jim had the qualities of what NJGO looks for in its members and continued to maintain these qualities to the day of his passing. We happily, yet sadly, recall that when Jim had attended one of Richard's lectures, when the lecture had ended, Karen hugged him and gave him a kiss goodbye, not knowing it would be the very last time we would see him. Alice still feels his presence and has had experiences since the morning of his funeral. We all agree that Jim now knows what we, as paranormal investigators keep trying to document and prove. Jim, please come and visit us often, we all miss you!

Acknowledgments

Richard and Karen would like to thank the current members of New Jersey Ghost Organization first and foremost for their friendship, dedication, honesty, integrity, and work ethic. We have been to some strange places and have seen some strange people on our somewhat unusual road trips, listening to, following up, and searching out the many folklore tales, all the while maintaining professionalism and meeting and helping some wonderful and appreciative clients.

We would also like to acknowledge our families, friends, and the families of our group members for allowing us to do what we do and the fact that they take an interest in what we do, helping wherever and whenever they can. We wish to thank the paranormal, as well as the other groups and individuals we have come to know and work with in our travels. Not to forget Jimmy at Asbury Pie, the best pizza on the Jersey Shore, for his help and understanding of why and what information we were seeking; Haunted Tales in Atlantic City for a welcome departure from the well-worn path of the paranormal; Paranormal Books & Museum for a superb collection of knowledge and for the representation of keeping folklore and the paranormal alive; and last but not least, the generosity of these people most of whom were once strangers and who we now consider our friends... Thank you all!

Foreword

The sense of history "being alive" comes to fruition in Richard and Karen's latest book. As people begin to explore their interest in the paranormal, they are often dazzled and confused by the array of electronic gizmos and gadgets that popular media has emphasized is a staple of any good ghost hunter. Popular culture does not emphasize the most basic building block of any haunted house, encounter with a mysterious creature or experience that an individual just cannot explain — a good story! It is that element which is passed down in the simplest of oral traditions from generation to generation; in turn, each person adding their own encounter along the way and becoming a piece of living history that becomes known as the "Folklore of the Jersey Shore."

Richard and Karen's obvious love of history is evident in every turn of the page. The stories they share are gripping, based in history and personal experiences, with some encounters shared from the "spiritual" perspective. We soon learn that ghost stories are not just for the living; the dead have stories that encourage readers to become part of that history as well.

— Author Dwayne Claud

Welcome to New Jersey

If you plan to visit New Jersey anytime soon, here are some humorous ways to tell us locals from the out-of-towner's...

- It's called Great Adventure, not Six Flags.
- The locals have known the way to Seaside Heights since they were seven.
- They know that the state isn't one big oil refinery.
- We know what a "jug handle" is.
- New Jerseyans know that there are no "beaches" here—there's the shore—and you don't go "to the shore," you go "down the shore." Also, when you are there, you're not "at the shore," you are "down the shore."
- Locals know that people from North Jersey go to Seaside Heights and people from Central Jersey go to Belmar and people from South Jersey go to Wildwood. That's just the way it is!
- Ask and you will find that not one of us was raised in New Jersey — we were raised in either North Jersey, Central Jersey, or South Jersey.
- We know how to properly negotiate a circle.
- The locals also know that the previous sentence had to do with driving!
- Finally, perhaps most important . . . **WE NEVER, EVER PUMP OUR OWN GAS!**

Me, My Dad, and NJGO

When my father first asked me to co-write this book with him, I have to admit I was a little nervous, as I had really never been involved with something of this magnitude before. I also felt that I did not want to intrude upon his successes with becoming a published author, as he did late in life at the age of seventy-three; he is now seventy-six. After giving some thought to what I have just said and when you consider it with what I am about to share with you, it did seem to make perfect sense that I accept his offer to co-write this book.

To give you a little background history, I founded my own paranormal group, New Jersey Ghost Organization (NJGO) almost nine years ago, during a time period before many of the paranormal shows you see on television now began flooding the television channels. For a long time, dad and I, actually since my early adulthood, had a great deal of interest in the paranormal and, as a gift on one of his birthdays, I bought two memberships to a local paranormal group, one for him and the other for myself; however, as it turned out, it was not what we really expected. This was now the beginning; a turning point for what would become a shared and very interesting endeavor for the both of us. Not only did my father do what most parents typically do, encourage their children, he also suggested that I start my own paranormal group, and dad, being a trained military photographer during the Korean conflict era, accompanies me on most of the group's investigations, taking most of the photographs. He always lends his help, advice, and opinions.

I am certain that you have heard the old sayings "people don't believe in something until they experience it themselves" or that "seeing is believing." This I have come to know as being so true and during my longevity at the helm of my group, we have encountered people with their own "ghostly" stories to share, which is one of the main reasons people join paranormal groups; my dad and I were no different, or so we thought. Over the years, even early on, dad and I would occasionally exchange independent instances of something that we had experienced, obviously with a little skepticism, but that could have been classified as being paranormal. It was not until we began our journey into the paranormal that this took an unusual turn.

On one occasion, after retiring for the night, I experienced in a dream that I was being led up a semi-circular driveway, flanked on both sides by two very small children holding my hands. To this day I am not able to distinguish if they were a boy(s) or a girl(s). As we approached the destination, I saw my paternal grandmother, who had passed away when I was just a teenager, standing near the bottom of what seemed like many steps of a very large, very white, columned, statuesque building, which seemed like it touched the sky. Picture if you will, a structure similar to the Lincoln Memorial or Capitol building in Washington, D.C., both of which are very important buildings. This scene seemed so strange to me because it was nothing that I recognized ever before in any dream; it didn't become clear to me until many years later what all this really meant, even though this was a recurring dream.

I have always enjoyed reading a good book. In the early years with NJGO, I would read a variety of books relating to the subject of the paranormal. I still do — after all delving into the paranormal is a never-ending process of education. One such book, authored by Sylvia Browne, a fairly well known psychic, was titled *Life on the Other Side*. As I read through this book, I learned what is believed to occur on the "other side" and it became clear that I had, or so it seemed, been to this "other side" in my dream — or was it a dream? Maybe I had actually traveled there? The building in my dream mirrored "The Hall of Records" described so vividly by Browne. I had mentioned earlier that the building I saw in my dream was an important building, and this building was described in her book as being the first place you go when you cross-over, the place where you review the life you just left here on this earth-plane. It had now become crystal clear that my grandmother will be the one that I see first waiting for me on the day when I finally take the journey myself.

As my experience continued, I recall recounting to my dad the conversation I had with my grandmother, as brief as it seemed. I did not hear her speak, but rather communicated her responses through thought. I was asking her where grandpa was, as he had passed away ten years after she had. My grandmother replied that he would be along any minute. When I looked toward the opposite side of this semi-circular driveway, I saw a vehicle that looked like an old pick-up truck coming toward me. Now I recall those two children that were holding my hand had long disappeared, most likely when my grandmother and I came face-to-face. The style of this truck was the kind you would see rusted and sitting on a farm somewhere in the Midwest. It wasn't rusted, but it had those high, rounded wheel fenders. I could not recall what color the truck was. It was indeed my grandfather at the wheel, waving his hand out the window as to greet me. He was smiling and, at this point, my experience concluded. When I have had this dream at other times, nothing seems to change very much and the best conclusion I can reach is simply that I am not ready to make my final journey or that I am not permitted to see more. To my surprise, I was about to find out that I was not the only one who has had this similar dream.

My dad had this very same dream, but with very slight differences that did not alter the total impact of the experience. In his dream, he is walking up this very same driveway, but without escorts. The building seems to be slightly on the grayish side, not white as in my dream, and the truck my grandfather is driving is a step-van, different than the kind he was driving in my dream. My dad later told me that back in the early 1900s, when my grandfather was in high school, he would earn extra money by driving an enclosed, horse-drawn wagon, delivering candy for a local store. So, as you can see, because of these similar experiences it made perfect sense for me co-write this book with my dad; after all, it seems that we may have been destined to be on this journey together.

Although it is sad to think about leaving loved ones one day, neither my dad nor myself are afraid to be on the other side. It appears that we were both privileged to have had a glimpse of it. After all it is what we, as well as others, have been attempting to prove — that the existence of life after death is another existence in another dimension.

In NJGO, we acknowledge how important it is to have supporting evidence to back-up anything we may get on camera: voice recorder, video, or any of the other handheld scientific instruments we use to record changes in room temperature, detect electromagnetic fields, and any personal experiences we may have while on an investigation. Working with psychics is something NJGO has believed in since the very onset of the group because I know that somehow we need to combine the scientific and the spiritual so that one day we will experience what we have believed in all along — the truth of life after death. Many segments of the folklore that you will encounter throughout this book include information from the case files of NJGO and some of the follow-up investigations surrounding them.

Folklore and legend are synonymous; the Brothers Grimm defined legend as "folktale historically grounded." A modern folklorist's professional definition of legend was proposed by Timothy R. Tangherlini in 1990: "Legend, typically, is a short (mono-episodic), traditional, highly ecotypified historicized narrative performed in a conversational mode, reflecting on a psychological level a symbolic representation of folk belief and collective experiences and serving as a reaffirmation of commonly held values of the group to whose tradition it belongs." In essence, this simply implies that folklore is merely an extension of one's imagination in combination with personal experiences, tiny pieces of history, minor or prominent, embellished as the story is passed on, and on, and on.

Keeping in mind the above definitions and explanation of folklore, let us now slip into our swimsuits, don our backpacks, climb into our automobile or mount our bicycle, and dive, hike, or drive into, and to, the lure of the oceans, trails, or roadways of *Folklore of the New Jersey Shore*!

Legends, Myths, and 'Oh My' – Ghosts!

In our quest, when researching many of the folklore stories for this work, we reached out to many of our associates and friends throughout the United States asking if they have ever heard of a folklore story emanating from the New Jersey shore area. Many who responded told us that they had and, much to our surprise, several of the stories were one in the same, as those that we had encountered during our lifetime living here in New Jersey. It amazed us that the folklore had spread to just about all four corners of the United States, including as far west as Hawaii. Most of the folklore encountered during our travels seemed to be of local genre, except for the ones that we have heard many times before.

Pirates, rumrunners, and rock 'n' roll are the foundations for myths treasured by locals for generations at the shore, stories that convince people they live in a special place.

Anti-German hysteria during World War I led to accusations that German-American sympathizers signaled U-boats lying offshore. Whispers arose that the German-owned Goldschmidt Wireless transmitter near Tuckerton transmitted intelligence that led to the 1916 sinking of the passenger liner *Luisitania* near Ireland and the deaths of more than 1,000 civilians including Americans.

Like all good folk history, the stories have a kernel of truth, glossed over with layers of fanciful veneer. Romantic anecdotes about the American Revolution and Prohibition conveniently leave out episodes of brutal violence.

Tales of German U-boats sneaking past Sandy Hook in shallow water defy common sense, but the submarines were a profound psychological weapon for having brought war to America's doorstep for two generations. Joseph Campbell, who popularized comparative mythology, famously observed, "It is never difficult to demonstrate that as science and history, mythology is absurd." However, Campbell also maintained that any society risks its spiritual roots if it insists on complete rationality in all its storytelling.

Folklore is traditional beliefs and stories. These are typically fictional in nature, tales about people and/or animals. You can include customs and practices, jokes, or songs that are told over and over, handed down from person-to-person, generation-to-generation. Folklore is rarely written down and over time the stories can slightly change, but they rarely stray from their origin. Legends, myths, ghost stories, and fairytales are also terms that seem to mean the same thing, but with slight differences. The common element seems to be people and/or animals.

While a myth is also a traditional story, it usually has biblical tones. It attempts to explain religious mysteries and both cultural and supernatural events in a very dramatic way, but still representing reality, Gods, and creatures. Legends are stories told as if they are a historical event in nature, but they're really not substantiated and are typically over-exaggerated and larger than life. An example of this is the legend of Robin Hood. Fairytales involve fairies, dragons, and elves to name a few and are typically told to children; twisted tales of slightly human, slightly animal, almost magical… people or horses with wings, for example. Ghost stories can be a little bit of these.

However, is folklore really fictional? Ask anyone from New Jersey and you may be surprised by his or her answer.

If you live or have ever lived in New Jersey or were just passing through, no doubt you have heard the words "Jersey Devil." New Jersey's national hockey league team is even called the Jersey Devils. There were movies made about the Jersey Devil, but have you ever heard about Captain Kidd, Blackbeard the pirate, or buried treasure in New Jersey? Some are considered legends as time moves forward, but has some folklore become reality? It's a grey area begging to be uncovered.

As paranormal investigators, we find that quite often investigations are initiated by claims based upon folklore and legends: stories passed down from generation to generation. It always raises the question when people report that they've seen and/or heard something they cannot explain and the Jersey Shore is no different. Folklore and the paranormal seem to run parallel to each other, similar in many aspects, mainly because of the fine membrane that separates or combines the other side and the story itself as it's passed down. Yet, time seems to have a unique way of standing still with frozen aspects of some almost long-forgotten times remaining in the forefront through the legends of *Folklore of the New Jersey Shore*.

After reading this book — a work not having been accomplished before with the paranormal twist that we have included — you may begin to realize that there is more to some of the folklore than you had ever imagined. The New Jersey Shore not only extends along the eastern coast of the state from Monmouth County South to its southern most point, Cape May, but up its western coastline along the Delaware River to Burlington County, dotted with many beaches, resorts, and marinas. It is simply not just the lure of the ocean; we would be negligent if we did not mention the lure of the many gambling casinos of Atlantic City. You will also discover that in some situations historical events have given birth to folklore.

Our hope is that our experiences and findings will help you to discover if folklore is just that, folklore, or that it is in part factual, ghostly activity bordering the supernatural or beyond.

The New Jersey Pinelands

The New Jersey Pinelands is a heavily forested, sandy, nutrient-poor soil coastal plain area. This uncommon and unusual area, as well as its condition, supports an odd variety of plant life: orchids and carnivorous plants, plus an abundance of cranberries and blueberries. Another unusual fact is the population of rare pigmy Pitch Pines that, believe it or not, rely on frequent forest fires in order to reproduce. These forest fires are a common occurrence.

Pine Barrens road to nowhere…

The Pine Barrens is largely rural despite the fact the Garden State Parkway and the Atlantic City Expressway run through them, but there are also smaller pockets of the Pine Barrens throughout Southern New Jersey.

Coupled with the fact that the Pine Barrens is home to approximately three hundred species of bird, fifty-nine species of reptiles and other amphibious creatures, thirty-nine species of mammals, and ninety-one species of fish, long ago the Pine Barrens was also possibly home to some less fortunate backwoods families having been lovingly dubbed the name "Pineys," a name that becomes a significant part of the foundation of some of the folklore in New Jersey. Only a part — the pre-colonial history — plays an important role in fostering the many stories and legends of the Garden State. Some of the roads within these pinelands lead nowhere and end at a tiny clearing... One can imagine what had once taken place here or is currently: satanic rituals, occult meetings, a whisky still.

In part, some of this may be the fiction weaving its way through and, as a finale, the paranormal aspect tying most of this together and forming the basis for this book.

Myth? You Decide!

From the northern shore to the southern beaches — with Central New Jersey's coastline in between — there is a cauldron of ghostly sightings. The following places are just a few to help you in discovering and experiencing New Jersey like you never have before. Please keep in mind that some of these locations may be private residences or have limited access to the public and require permission. Happy Hunting!

Devil's Tower, Cape May. A man built the tower so his wife could see the New York City Skyline. The only problem was that she saw more than what she bargained for! She saw her husband with another woman. It has been said by many people that if you circle the tower three times you will see "something." I guess you will have to find out for yourself.

Taj Mahal Casino Parking Garage, Atlantic City: A man apparently committed suicide by jumping or falling from the tenth floor of the parking deck. If you go there at midnight, you just may see him.

Burlington County Prison Museum, Mt. Holly: On the third floor is Cell No. 5, where Joseph Clough and soldiers from World Wars I and II were held. During the fall months, you can hear sounds of running feet on the leaves.

Fort Dix's "Haunted Hospital": This hospital has seen its share of wartime victims and the basement of the hospital is where the morgue was located. At times the spirits of some of the hospital's past residents can be seen peering from the windows, presenting visitors with a feeling that there is someone watching them. Repeated sightings, noises, and furniture being thrown around on the top five floors have been reported.

Castle Park, Toms River: On clear, calm nights, unusual phenomena are said to take place at midnight with all the swings swaying in rhythm at the same time without any sign of wind being present. Some have claimed that you can hear the sounds of children playing when no one is around. Castle Park is located near the Dover Township Police complex by the Bay Lea Golf Course. Should you plan on being here at midnight some dark moonlit night, I would suggest that you let the police know why and what you will be doing.

Ancora, New Jersey Veterans Haven: Situated right next to the Bayside Prison Ward and Ancora mental institution, this was once a town that the psychiatric hospital made for patients to all live together and it was there that many of the patients murdered each other, most of whom were old veterans. Eventually so many killings had taken place that the whole town was simply shut down. There is still a great deal of paranormal activity and unusual as it may seem the streetlights are still left on throughout this little-known deserted ghost town.

Animal Ghosts

You cannot discuss the paranormal without discussing animals and what happens to them when they pass on. Our experience with animal spirits on investigations is very much alive and well. It appears to be very common to experience these types of phenomena, especially first-hand after losing such a beloved pet, personally speaking.

The same rules apply when it comes to dealing with hauntings — most of our experiences are residual in nature. We believe very strongly that animals have souls and for that matter feelings and emotions. Animals feel pain and joy. Ask yourself when you have more than one pet and one dies, haven't you noticed that the pet that remains reacts in ways that perhaps they miss the deceased one? How about when the pet owner dies and the animal remains? The bond between man and animal is so strong that it must transcend death, right? Until there is definitive proof that a life form must possess a soul in order to come back, then this decision rests with how you feel towards animals.

Some of what we as paranormal investigators encounter is obvious; for example, an animal's strong bond with a particular location. We investigated what was once a private eccentric's residence, now a private lodge. One of the many claims of paranormal activity was the sighting of a cat roaming the building. During the course of the evening we conducted a séance, not with the cat in mind, but at one point several members of our team experienced nuzzling around their ankles, like what a cat does. When we reviewed video following this investigation, we spotted a single orb moving very low to the ground at the same time the nuzzling was reported.

I had a first-hand experience of this in my own home about six months after our cat passed away. By the way she was almost twenty-three years old at the time of her death. Every so often I would see something out of the corner of my eye in what was a favorite spot for the cat to rest, on top of the couch. I would see movement as if she was hopping down onto the floor and then either see movement by the kitchen doorway or a little further in the hallway. It never bothered me in the least; after all, I go into many haunted locations and face the unknown. One day I was showering and I had the feeling that someone had quietly entered the bathroom. Thinking that it was perhaps the dog nosing the door open to come and sit on the rug, I called his name. Usually at this point you would see his head poke through the shower curtain. That did not happen. What I did see was a shadow (of the four-legged kind) moving slowly past the shower curtain. Now my interest peaked and I looked out. The bathroom door was shut tight and no signs of the dog, actually no signs of anything. What I saw was the size of the cat, or dog for that matter, and the shadow that was moving in front of the curtain would have been the cat walking directly towards where her litter box was. Thinking back to the morning she died, I think that she knew it was going to be her last day with us. Twenty-three years old. Hell, most marriages don't last that long! In all of those years, that special bond between man and animal — the bond we had with her would be something to reckon with — and so many years of coming into the bathroom, so many years of hopping down from the couch top and walking into the kitchen for food and water... It would be hard not to miss.

One of our team members had a similar experience. Their beloved cat passed on, but this time they took a proactive approach and decided to photograph the familiar places the cat frequented. In the member's photographs was a single orb on top of the pillow on the bed. The cat's bed was in the closet and a single orb appeared in the photograph. These were the cat's favorite places to snooze.

Despite an ever-opposing view, these experiences translate to a sense of comfort in knowing this special bond can never be broken between man and their pet. I find comfort, as I am sure many people do, in the poem called "The Rainbow Bridge."

> Just this side of heaven is a place called Rainbow Bridge.
> When an animal dies that has been especially close to someone here, that pet goes to Rainbow Bridge. There are meadows and hills for all of our special friends so they can run and play together. There is plenty of food, water and sunshine, and our friends are warm and comfortable.
> All the animals who had been ill and old are restored to health and vigor. Those who were hurt or maimed are made whole and strong again, just as we remember them in our dreams of days and times gone by. The animals are happy and content, except for one small thing; they each miss someone very special to them, who had to be left behind.
> They all run and play together, but the day comes when one suddenly stops and looks into the distance. His bright eyes are intent. His eager body quivers. Suddenly he begins to run from the group, flying over the green grass, his legs carrying him faster and faster.
> You have been spotted, and when you and your special friend finally meet, you cling together in joyous reunion, never to be parted again. The happy kisses rain upon your face; your hands again caress the beloved head, and you look once more into the trusting eyes of your pet, so long gone from your life but never absent from your heart.
> Then you cross Rainbow Bridge together.
>
> -- Author unknown

When my neighbor's dog passed away, I found the most befitting sympathy card that says it all: "Your pet was a wonderful companion and friend, and it's understandably hard to say goodbye. Please know that you did all you could to provide such a sweet animal with a good life and a happy home."

There is much controversy with the argument of whether or not animals have souls, which is based on the assumption that you need to have emotions in order to have a soul. We strongly believe that as pet owners we have had the experience of a very warm and very real relationship with our beloved pets. Indeed we have witnessed emotion. We witness anger, happiness, hunger, pain, and recognize when an animal feels the loss of their human or another pet in the household.

Our belief is that one day our time will come when we reunite with our pets in spirit and they will be waiting for us.

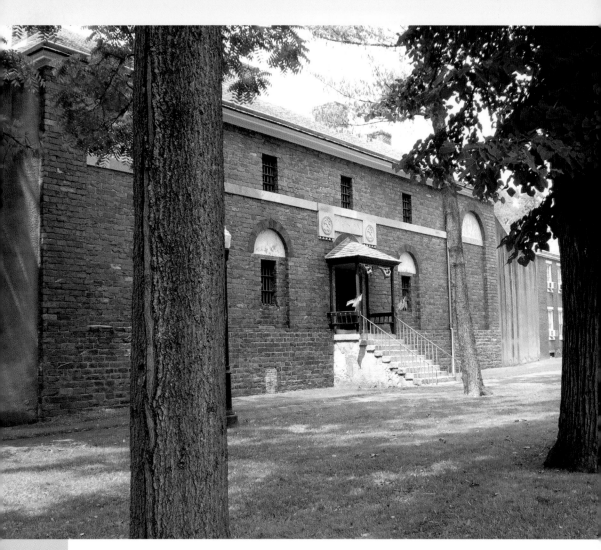

Exterior view of Burlington County Prison Museum,
Mt. Holly, New Jersey.

Chapter 1

A 'Haunting' We Will Go

A stone's throw from the western coastline of New Jersey, in Burlington County, is a location that houses all aspects of what has been mentioned so far — folklore, legend, ghostly activity, the supernatural, and beyond: the Burlington County Prison Museum.

To preface this chapter, whenever the New Jersey Ghost Organization investigates a haunted location or a purportedly haunted location, we try to research and evaluate the historical background of the location beforehand. The novice, as well as the more experienced investigator, should always keep this research factor in mind, and I am certain that they would agree that this is a more common sense approach to consider before one can intelligently proceed with a proper investigation. People who work or live in a place day in and day out are much more certain of what they are claiming to be experiencing, even though we, as a professional group, are not until we actually investigate the claims. It is important to focus on the specific areas of where these claims originate, because why waste valuable time on areas that have not been reported as having paranormal activity or are "not active," right? Wrong! One must consider the entire location since spirit activity may avail itself at any time and any where.

As a group, having always been dedicated to discovering the truth, we strongly believe in working closely with psychics on our investigations. We will never share information about a specific location with a psychic beforehand, for obvious reasons, and a good psychic prefers to "go in cold" on an investigation. It is just a more common sense approach that will support any evidence gathered while on an investigation.

The investigation we are about to take you through will hopefully amaze you as much as the final outcome amazed us. Perhaps you will even find some of the aspects amusing.

Burlington County Prison

Now a museum and historical landmark, the prison is located in historic Mt. Holly, New Jersey. The completion of the building was accomplished in 1811 and remained in use as a prison until 1965, an impressive 154 years. One can imagine not only the many prisoners who have walked through these doors, but also who they were, the crimes they had been incarcerated for, and what fate had in store for them. This was the type of prison where executions were consummated by hangings in the prison yard. The last such hangings were of two men, Rufus Johnson and George Small, simultaneously convicted of murdering Florence Allinson of Moorestown. Florence worked as a governess at a local establishment for homeless children. Another instance was that of an individual by the name of Albert DeSalvo, who, while serving in the Army at nearby Fort Dix, was on a day pass and had spent time here at BCP for allegedly raping a woman. The alleged victim failed to appear in court and he was released. After he completed his enlistment, he later became known as the infamous Boston Strangler. In another instance, famous detective Ellis Parker believed he had the real kidnapper of the Lindbergh baby brought to this prison and it was not Bruno Hauptmann, who had been the accused in this tragedy.

All of this information was not originally known to our investigative group, much less the stories of workers who experienced strange, unexplainable, happenings at the location, until we made our first visit to the prison. There are hundreds, if not thousands, of places in New Jersey waiting to be explored and it is nearly impossible to know of each and every place, and I will be the first to freely admit this. I know that when speaking and sharing information with other groups, you eventually find out that they too have trodded the sinister corridors of the Burlington County Prison Museum. Living in any state, inclusive of New Jersey, and having the Internet so readily available, you can certainly find websites listing "haunted places," but are these places really haunted? Even far back in our childhood memories, we heard talk of haunted places and recall a few that had been definitely placed on our list for future investigations. We are also firm believers in that timing is everything, and when you read and see what we have discovered at the prison... well, you will simply have to act as your own judge and jury.

The Investigation

Upon our many visits to the Burlington County Prison Museum, we were greeted by an employee who served as our guide; whether you are a visitor or a paranormal group, the initial visit is no different. Our guide gave us a brief overview of the history of the prison, its purposes and functionality, and some of the highlighted events that occurred during its 154 years of operation. Mostly the prison was really no different than any other prison; attempted jailbreaks, suicides, differences of opinion, racial differences, and other things of this nature, but when you add in murder... Now it begins to get really interesting.

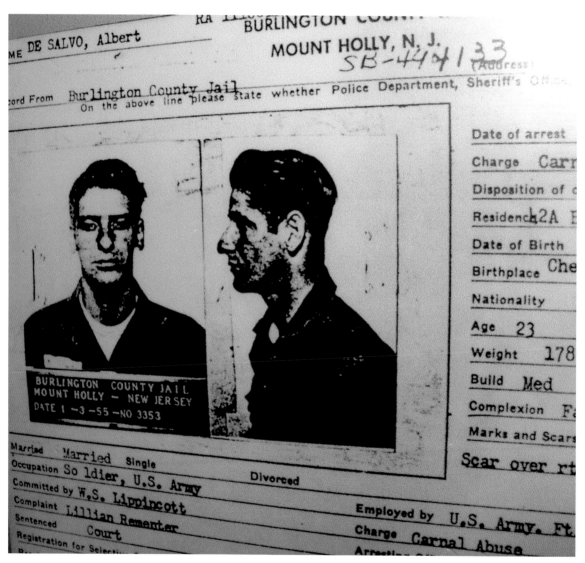

Original Burlington County Prison file card of the infamous Boston Strangler when he was being detained for an earlier unrelated local crime while serving in the U.S. Army stationed at Fort Dix, New Jersey.

Touring the prison, as with most historic places, there is information on plaques and signs throughout its three floors. Though a psychic certainly is exposed to this information, they are not privy to any stories of activity or experiences of the paranormal. From this point on, I will give you an overview of the culmination of our many visits and, hopefully, you will see how our psychic's impressions and the evidence intertwined to give us the results we obtained. Not each visit required a psychic to be there with us and you will understand that as well.

One of our psychics on this particular visit picked up on many names, one of which was "John Holman" — and the feeling she got was that he was a spirit that did not respect women at all. When the prison looked through their logbooks, our guide only found one John — John Holmes — and he seemed to fit what our psychic said. Holmes served time for vagrancy. It's a huge undertaking for the prison to go through old logbooks and, as it was an ongoing project, had already gone through 9,000 prisoners' names and entered them into a computer database.

Another interesting experience to point out was that one of the cells had a bathtub at one time, which was removed and covered over with a piece of plywood. Both the psychic and team members experienced vertigo while standing on the plywood. The guide explained that when the bathtub was functional the inmates stood on it for leverage to climb on each other's shoulders to escape through a corner in the ceiling. Not all of the inmates were successful. When we left and went home to review our photographs, audio, and video, we were extremely proud of a job well done.

One of the events that occurred at the prison involved an inmate named Harry Asay. Originally his incarceration was for stealing tires. Eighteen years later, when he returned as a repeat offender, it was for being drunk and disorderly. It was during this particular incarceration that Harry Asay's only goal upon entering prison life again was to kill a prison guard. It is our understanding that how he committed this horrific murder was with a fireplace poker obtained from the Kitchen cell, which is approximately two double cells and a single cell away from the corner in which Asay's cell was located. The guard was ambushed and bludgeoned to death, along with another prisoner, and dragged to a position that was out of site. Upon reviewing our possible evidence, we had video of an anomalous shape moving across the tape — very self-luminous. At the same time, a very sinister male laugh came through on the audio... Both of these came from the exact location where the guard was ambushed and murdered. This particular guard turned out to be the Prison Warden Harry King. We believe we recorded a small part of this event. The locations were right and the team had left the basement while the video and audio were in use. This particular visit was also a learning experience. When we got home and looked over our photographs, we discovered a huge faux pas. Not with what we had already captured on video and audio, but what we picked up on one of the still cameras.

Testing the Evidence

At first glance the photograph appears to have captured one of the prison's spirits, a long-ago resident, during a session in the main hallway of the prison's lower level. The excitement this capture caused when reviewing the many still photographs taken that evening was off the charts, as full-body images recorded during investigations are extremely scarce and you might even say rare! Was this a coincidence that we were at the right place at the right time? At first we had thought this was the case, but we have been to this location several times during past investigations and felt that we were known to the spirits still dwelling there, so one would think that we would have made this type of capture prior to this visit.

Alas, after extensive examination, we discovered, to our extreme disappointment, that what was actually captured was not what we had first thought. We felt that we now had to return to the prison — to the exact location — in an attempt to recreate the circumstances surrounding this capture, if for no other reason than to be absolutely certain before making the image public.

We returned to the prison early one afternoon to review what we had done a week or so earlier. There were other visitors there at the time; however, their presence would not interfere with what we were about to do. Richard immediately went to the basement and the vicinity where he had taken the initial photograph of what we thought was the spirit image. Once again, the camera was attached to a tripod facing the exact area to hopefully recreate the previous photograph. As before, the shutter of the camera was set for a ten-second time exposure and the flash was turned off. Taking the same position behind the camera, the exposure began.

During this experiment one of our members had positioned himself in the area where members of the group had initially been sitting with their red-lens flashlights on while another member began flashing his camera several times during the same time that Richard was making the test time exposure. We were able to see that a shadow from the flash was being cast down the hallway and partially on the side of one of the arches near where Richard was standing. After doing this same experiment several times, we packed up and left for home to check our results.

While reviewing the test exposures, we noticed that the shadow that we had seen of Richard did not appear in any of the photographs. Photographically this is very plausible, as the shadow of Richard that was created by the camera flash that was behind him was extremely brief and would not have been recorded. However, during the initial investigation, with the group sitting in the rear with their red lights glowing steadily during the original ten-second exposure, combined with Richard not having moved, his shadow would, in fact, be recorded. The only conclusion that one might reach is what we first thought was a spirit image was actually the image of Richard's shadow being cast forward.

In re-staging the shadow image, we discovered that the original shadow image was that of Richard himself.

The Basement

Since we were fascinated with the basement from the evidence of the first visit, we thought we would like to try different types of equipment in hopes of capturing more of this horrific murder on camera, but we had very little luck, actually no luck at all.

One of our visits produced on video an orb that appeared to have come out of the wall heading at a very fast pace — it was coming straight towards one of our Infrared cameras, which was set up at the end of the hall. When we looked closely, the area from which the high-density orb came was a display on the wall showcasing the double hanging of Rufus Johnson and George Small.

It was not until a later visit that things started to heat up. We brought along another psychic, the renowned Psychic Jane Doherty, who picked up on similar situations that the first psychic picked up on and in the same areas, including outside in front of the prison a procession of horses and carriages that appeared to be something of importance. This could have been due to the newly formed State Police, Governor Hoffman, a hanging, and a funeral procession. Maybe it had something to do with the Lindbergh events and famed detective Ellis Parker or, in retrospect, the murder of Warden Harry King? Moving onto the Warden's Office and the immediate areas once inside the prison, both psychics picked up on pipe smoke. Ellis Parker smoked a pipe.

Unbeknownst to the psychics who accompanied us on our visits, we knew that children were a part of prison life. It is our understanding that occasionally if a husband was incarcerated, then the wife and children stayed at the prison too; most likely because they could not fend for themselves without any source of income. Team members experienced little tugs on clothing. In Jane Doherty's case, her paranormal stomach reacts to such sensations — whenever in the company of a spirit presence, her stomach will expand to a disproportionate size. There is no medical explanation for it. Jane senses when a child is around because her stomach only contracts to half of what it would normally expand to: the size of a child's stomach.

Both psychics at different times experienced similarities on the second floor's north end. Subsequently at this end there is a cell where several suicides occurred, and both psychics came to the same conclusions about the cell with the bathtub.

The Women's Wing is not a place to be overlooked. Jane felt that a female prisoner was raped by a guard and gave birth. The baby was smothered and tossed out the window by prison staff. She hears screaming (a woman's voice), beatings, taunting and teasing, and sees a female naked. Our guide confirmed that women prisoners were frequently paraded around, naked, and humiliated. Another psychic on another visit sees a female spirit who appeared to be lost there and didn't belong. On the video camera, we noticed three distinct orbs coming fast from one of the cells and, shortly thereafter, we hear the camera actually shutting off with a click and then turning on again with a click. Perhaps it was the people involved with the raping of the female prisoner and they did not want us to see what was happening?

There is also an area of the basement that we still have not concluded completely: the Workshop. Both psychics have seen a black man running away from the workshop down the hall. We have also captured on camera orbs at the foot of the stairs. We have a feeling this relates to the murder of Warden Harry King.

A Brutal Murder

During Jane's visit, we revisited the basement. Knowing that Jane's stomach reacts when there is spirit presence, we entered the basement end of where the murder of the Warden took place. She sees an active spirit that lurks or walks in this area. She feels it could be Warden King. The previous psychic was mentally and physically startled in this same area and saw in her mind a bright flash of red light. Something went on here and it had to be something big for more than one psychic to react so strongly. Getting back to Jane, her stomach starts to react and we followed a path twice to be sure what was happening. We followed the path all the way down the hall, past the Kitchen cell and the workshop by about two feet, which now takes us to the corner where Harry Asay's cell was. Jane's stomach returns to normal. We also did this in reverse and the same thing happened — stomach out near the workshop and continues all the way down the hall, returning to normal just before a cell at the other end (which is now a public men's bathroom).

Is this Warden King reliving his last stroll before he was killed? As King approached the Workshop doorway, Asay jumped out and ambushed the guard. He struck him with the fireplace poker that he got from the Kitchen cell, delivered the fatal blow to the Warden's head, and attempted to drag him around the corner right in front of his cell, also killing another prisoner Charles Bartlett in the process. It's possible that the reason Jane's stomach reacts to this path is because it is a residual haunting being replayed over and over again.

We take Jane to Harry Asay's cell. She immediately feels isolation and repulsion. Suddenly, her stomach reacts directly in front of Asay's cell. She sees pacing, adjuration. A murderer, a tough one and still mean, acts up in the spirit sense. She states that the guards had to be very careful with and around him, as she felt that he could overtake any one of them at anytime. He was incarcerated here, but not for murder. He was a repeat offender; he was beyond rehabilitation, locked up for something else. He was a mastermind, like a caged animal, a mental schizophrenic. She sees brute, blunt force.

After Jane has relayed her impressions, we finally explained to her the history of what had actually taken place here.

During Jane's visit, and with the permission of the prison guide, we decided to conduct a séance. Jane immediately sees the Warden — and just as immediately one of our video cameras shuts off even though a lot of time remains on the battery. An extreme coldness is felt by all of us in the room just prior to the video camera shutting off and then Jane sees the Warden standing directly in front of her. Now the guard's cold breeze is felt by some of the team on their cheeks while most of us feel it on our arms. Another video camera's battery drains. At one point Jane feels like she is being choked. The prisoner conveyed to her that he didn't do it. More than one team member felt pain in the neck. The prison guide confirmed a prisoner was indeed framed. It turned out to be the prisoner's uncle and another person who committed the crime he was convicted of. At one point, Jane saw the Warden standing behind her with his arms crossed: he was anxious to know why we were here.

Is it possible to experience a residual haunting and an active spirit as one in the same at the same location? Honestly, we don't know. Thus, there are always some unanswered questions that make paranormal investigators like us continue our research.

Halloween Hoax or Real Spirit?

Fast forward to an annual event that the prison hosts every fall, around Halloween: a haunted house type event where volunteers act out gruesome scenes and people pay an admission to be scared out of their wits. NJGO usually attends this event, as well as other groups, to promote themselves, hand out flyers, and possibly have positive evidence of paranormal activity on display for the public to see. The event takes place in the prison yard. At this event a couple of years ago we were startled while viewing random photos that one of our team members had taken while we were outside in front of the prison near where we had our table setup. The first one was of a team member sitting behind our table with her hands on her lap. A very bright high density-moving orb was on her hand. When the photo was snapped, she said she felt unusually cold. When viewing another photo, it seemed to look a little strange, but we could not quite put our finger on why it gave us this impression. In the back of my mind, I thought that her face did not quite look right. It was a photo of my dad and me in conversation with a couple of NJGO members standing slightly off to the side. When the member who took the photo showed us a zoomed in close-up of the photo, a short distance off in the background, there it was — a skull like figure in what appeared to be a dark robe was visible. Our first reaction was it might have been one of the volunteers in costume, but that was wrong since the feet of this figure were not touching the ground! Certainly, if it were a costume mask, there would be eyeholes or something else to indicate that it was a mask. It was almost as if there was a crowd of people…the crowd was parting and there this figure was. It did not seem real, but how and why? Somehow, the reason for this image had to be resolved; now came the importance for the intervention of a proven psychic.

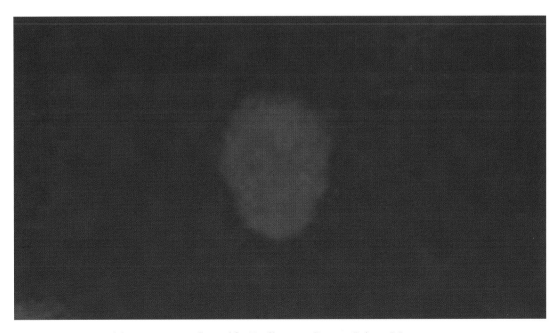

Supernatural image captured outside Burlington County Prison Museum.
Photo courtesy of Richard Wisenfelder.

The Analysis

We knew by the many visits we made to the prison the evidence we had gotten could be backed up, checked, balanced, and double-checked. However, this figure made no sense to us at all. We were not on an investigation at the time; we were outdoors with many people around. We decided that we had to have the psychics we work with take a look at the photo and not tell them anything…just have them take a cold look. The following are the results.

This was something bordering on the supernatural, something that we had not experienced on any of our previous investigations at the prison. Through psychic intervention we discovered that the image we captured was actually one of two entities that were about to do battle. Was it good versus evil or evil versus evil — and where was the second entity? As I mentioned earlier, the look on my face was not my normal face; it appeared that there was some sort of veil in front of it that the psychic saw. The second entity was actually behind the team member taking the photo. Now we became really curious as to just who these entities were? Since we could only see one in the photo, Jane was asked who she thought it was. If she looked at the characteristics of the skull, could she visualize the physical makeup of what the entity may have looked like in life? Jane's reply was immediate: "A strong person, large individual." This description could have easily fit Harry Asay, the prisoner that murdered Warden King. After all, during Asay's incarcerations, we know he was a force to be reckoned with. We do not know who the other entity is, most likely because it was not captured in the photo and it was something that the psychics could not see.

This discovery definitely opened the door to additional research — we had to know what this all meant. Always keep in mind that you can never move forward until you know the history of the location or of the individuals that you may be dealing with. These types of things just do not normally show up on camera. This was not the typical situation that we were used to seeing in our photographs, not some skull-like figure floating. No, we are used to seeing more human like apparitions in our photos.

To further our research, we start by looking at the weather conditions prevalent that evening. We backtracked a bit and later made note of the moon phases or any solar flares that day — anything that a good paranormal investigator would and should normally do. However, this was not a normal situation…or was it? After additional research, what we discovered was startling. We had been at the prison for this annual event on November 1, 2008, and the murders we spoke of had taken place on November 5, 1920. This was eighty-eight years ago and almost to the day, just about a four-day difference, but possibly not. We were there on a Saturday, so we began to look a bit further.

The final question is why was this skull-like entity outdoors, in front, and not within the security walls of the prison yard? Considering all of the circumstances, our research showed that after Asay killed both Warden King and fellow prisoner Charles Bartlett, he was never prosecuted for the crime. He was sent to an insane asylum in Trenton, New Jersey, so he was not serving time in the prison at this time and this we believe is the reason his image was captured outside.

An Intriguing Incident

My father and I went back to the prison recently to take some outdoor photos. In one of the photos that was taken from the outside of the warden's residence, a building that is attached to the prison's north side, the image of Warden King and a female were captured in one of the windows. This was totally unexpected as the photographs were being taken simply for record purposes; however, one should never look a gift-horse in the mouth!

Exterior view of warden's home and Burlington County Prison. In one of the close-up images, a face was captured in the second floor window (where arrow is indicating).

Chapter 2

Lindbergh Baby — Alive and Well?

Not more than thirty minutes from the beginning of the Jersey Shore coastline, in East Amwell, New Jersey, was the home Charles Augustus Lindbergh (February 4, 1902 – August 26, 1974). Nicknamed "Lucky Lindy" and "The Lone Eagle," Lindbergh was an American aviator, author, inventor, explorer, and social activist. Lindbergh, then a 25-year-old U.S. Air Mail pilot, emerged from virtual obscurity to almost instantaneous world fame as the result of his Orteig prize-winning solo non-stop flight on May 20-21, 1927, from Roosevelt Field located in Garden City on New York's Long Island to Le Bourget Field in Paris, France, a distance of nearly 3,600 statute miles in the single-seat, single-engine monoplane *Spirit of St. Louis*. Lindbergh, a U.S. Army reserve officer, was also awarded the nation's highest military decoration, the Medal of Honor, for his historic exploit.

Lindbergh's son, Charles Jr., was kidnapped on March 1, 1932. At the time, this blond hair, blue-eyed toddler was only nearing his second birthday. No doubt, the motive behind this horrendous crime was money and it was considered the crime of the century. This is a historical fact and, as alluded to earlier, more often than not folklore is historically grounded, even if only in slight ways.

It was about two months later that a trucker discovered a small body in nearby Hopewell, not more than two miles from the Lindbergh home. However, the discovery turned out to be the remains of a body and had marked decomposition, making it difficult, if not impossible, to determine the sex of the child. However, in what could be considered strange, if not suspicious, was that the corpse was quickly cremated after the Lindberghs' nanny identified the body. It was also discovered that the remains found did not match the height of the Lindbergh baby. The subsequent arrest and trial of an illegal German immigrant from New York City, Bruno Hauptmann, grabbed much attention and headlines worldwide. Even though Hauptmann was found guilty of kidnapping and murder, it is believed that the real murderer was already being held at the Burlington County Prison in Mount Holly, New Jersey.

Mount Holly itself is no stranger to evil. As we saw in Chapter One, many notorious criminals have called Burlington County Prison home! Back to the Lindbergh case, it is widely believed that the then newly-formed New

Jersey State Police needed to establish credibility and the slim leads that they had in the Lindbergh case were going nowhere. They were under the microscope to solve this kidnapping as quickly as possible. If they didn't, then they, along with New Jersey's then-Governor Hoffman, would be considered an embarrassment. The light at the end of the tunnel was that Hauptmann seemed to be an easy fix to their difficult situation. Supposedly, he was in possession of one of the ransom bills. In addition, a large sum of the ransom money was found hidden in his garage, but where was the remainder of the $50,000 in gold certificates? Hauptmann was executed in 1936 and the case was closed — or was it? Charles Lindbergh, less than two months prior to the actual kidnapping, had staged, what turned out to be, a hoax by reporting his son missing to his family and, to this day, no one knows why.

Fingerprint evidence gathered from baby Lindbergh's toys eventually and mysteriously disappeared, so where is the Lindbergh baby? Many people from all over the globe have claimed to be the real Lindbergh baby and should the Lindbergh baby still be alive he would be turning eighty years old this year. Considering that newspapers throughout the world were chomping at their bits for the capture of the killer and a conviction, were the authorities in New Jersey grasping at the straws of evidence in this case? Were they succumbing to the pressures of the world-press or were they simply listening to what was emanating from the lips of the locals? The whole truth may never be told and may have crossed over as well on the lips of the aviator himself. We may never know, but the stories and folklore will continue to live on!

Chapter 3

No Stranger to Evil

In the fall of 1730, a Philadelphia, Pennsylvania newspaper article spoke of a witch trial that had taken place just a stone's throw away in the New Jersey town of Mount Holly. As the story went, and has been retold over the years with added embellishments, a witch and a wizard stood trial, accused of practicing witchcraft, at the persistence of a few hundred residents who claimed their animals began behaving strangely. The accused were forced to undergo tests similar to the infamous Salem Witch Trials that had taken place in Massachusetts back in 1692. It was simple reasoning, at the time: If you weighed more than a stack of bibles, you were considered guilty. The townspeople still were not convinced, so they performed another test. The man and woman who stood accused had their hands and feet tied with rope and were placed in a nearby pond: If you were guilty, you would float to the top of the water's surface. To the townspeople's satisfaction, the two accused floated to the water's surface, pretty much sealing their fate of what was to come. There was only one problem — there was never a follow-up article in the Philadelphia newspaper to complete the story and its outcome.

Some continue to say that because the article was generated by a Pennsylvania newspaper that it is possible this all was the handiwork of Benjamin Franklin at the expense of the people of the town of Mount Holly simply because Franklin perhaps did not believe in the Witch Trials or, for that matter, witchcraft and he did not like these locals. It would appear that those events had never taken place and that this entire, alleged situation was a colossal hoax—or was it? Apparently, the residents of Mount Holly believe this series of events did indeed happen simply because the story has been passed down through the generations and into the annals of folklore.

Mount Holly and the Burlington County area have not just been the butt of Benjamin Franklin's apparent schoolboy hoax, there have been numerous reports of the fabled Jersey Devil sightings throughout this very historic and one of the oldest areas, being founded in 1688, in the western coastal shore area of New Jersey. It was not until 1909 that a surge of Jersey Devil sightings occurred in Mount Holly and stories of mysterious hoof prints in the snow and the hideous piercing scream of this mythical creature surfaced. Almost every yard in Burlington claimed to have experienced these mysterious hoof prints and anyone from police officers to pastors, even notable government officials, have claimed to witness this cryptid.

Chapter 4

Taking a Bite out of Life

When all the elements of a story come together — historical fact, fiction, mystery, missing pieces to the puzzle — and then you add a bit of the paranormal to it, the mix spawns folklore. I am certain that you will find the 'lure' of this tale too much to resist a visit to the area.

Living in New Jersey we have the luxury of both the mountains in Sussex County to the beaches from the famous Asbury Park, as sung by Bruce Springsteen, to the most southern tip of historic Cape May. My dad and I, both lifelong residents of New Jersey, recall just about each and every summer hearing and reading of shark sightings at the local beaches and, for that matter, up and down the entire East Coast, from pretty much New York to Florida. If you live in New Jersey, it's typical each summer. If you don't live in New Jersey, it sounds pretty scary, don't you think? However, what would you say if you heard news of shark sightings smack in the middle of Central New Jersey? How about what ended in a New Jersey creek? No way, right?

We are sure that is what residents in Matawan, New Jersey, said back in July 1916. Never had there been such terror unleashed in the history of New Jersey. Some refer to July 1st to July 12th as twelve days of terror and the worst shark attacks in U.S. history. This all happened with possibly a single shark roaming from Beach Haven in the Keyport area and Spring Lake to Matawan Creek. The month of July 1916 reminded me of how July 2010 was: brutally hot and humid and oppressive heat. No one could imagine what was about to happen in this quiet little town. Imagine a shark sneaking in virtually undetected until it was too late. For twenty-four hours a valiant effort was in place to shoot at, stab, and dynamite this shark dubbed the Matawan Beast. Was this beast the only one? After all, there was a great white caught only two weeks earlier in Perth Amboy, New Jersey, filled with human flesh. Is it possible the victims whose lives were cut so abruptly short still remain in spirit in the town they call home? Let's back up a little to see what happened in the summer of 1916.

One "Great White" Summer

With such a hot, humid, oppressive summer already beginning and with July Fourth quickly approaching, many people were flocking to the Jersey Shore to the cool refreshing waters of the Atlantic Ocean. People not on vacation and hard at work took every opportunity to cool off in any water they could find. Already before July 12th two people were dead; one aged twenty-five, the other twenty-eight. However, these incidents were probably not on the minds of Matawan's youth.

Twelve-year-old Joseph Dunn from New York City was visiting his aunt in Matawan and swimming at the Clay Company brickyard docks on the north side of the Matawan Creek when he was attacked. He survived with a leg amputation. After his leg was mauled, he was taken to Saint Peter's Hospital in New Brunswick, New Jersey. There was also Lester Stillwell, another twelve-year-old who worked for a local basket factory during the summer. Lester and his friends were enjoying the cool water at the Wyckoff dock. Stanley Fisher, a local dry cleaner, was killed trying to save Lester, whose legs were missing when he finally surfaced a couple of days later upstream near the railroad trestle. Stanley's injuries on his leg made it necessary to be transported by train to a hospital in Long Branch, New Jersey; he died a short time later.

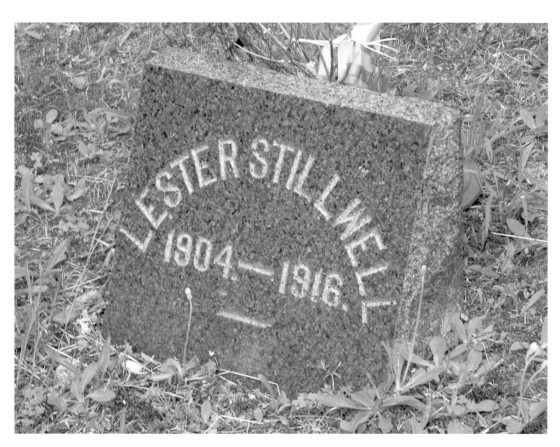

Gravesite of Lester Stillwell, shark attack victim – the site is in Rosehill cemetery.

Rosehill Cemetery is the final resting place for Captain Thomas Cottrell, who killed "a" shark about three days after Lester Stillwell and Stanley Fisher were buried.

The Investigation

New Jersey Ghost Organization has made a few trips to Rosehill Cemetery, some during the day and some at night, but always around the "anniversary" week of the shark attacks. The cemetery is located just off of the main road and surrounded by residential neighborhoods. Because of the natural sounds that normally occur from neighbors talking loud, especially at night, any noise or sound seem to be amplified and travel long distances, lending little help when attempting to do EVPs (voice recordings). A cemetery in general also doesn't help our psychics because it can seem like the dead can vie for their attention sometimes. There are times when we simply rely solely on our cameras, smaller handheld equipment, and personal experiences. In the past we have also ventured to Rosehill with another paranormal group.

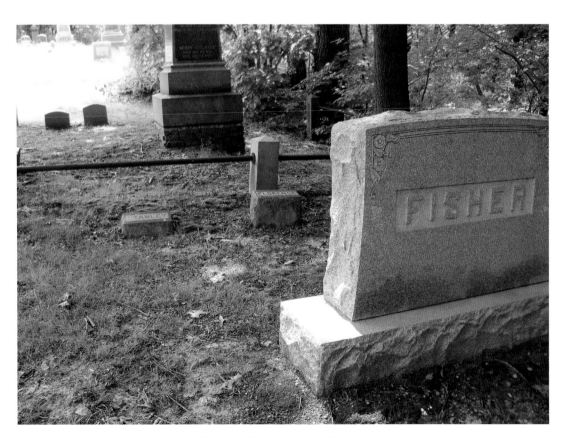

Gravesite of Watson Stanley Fisher — its location has been virtually unknown until now. Site is in Rosehill Cemetery.

Rosehill, although not a terribly large cemetery, after the sun goes down, seems to take on a whole different persona. The back section of the cemetery goes slightly upgrade and loops around diminishing to different levels. In the dark, it seems as though it is easy to get oneself a little disoriented, if only for a brief minute. On a couple of occasions we were able to locate the graves of several individuals of the "shark attack" era, only to miss the location when we returned a few minutes later, leading to some confusing "over here, no they are over here." Watson Stanley Fisher's gravesite in Rosehill has been rumored over the years to be "missing"; however, knowledge of its location seems to be known by very few, including NJGO.

Lester Stillwell's grave has flowers placed on it once a year. Imagine, twelve years old and died so tragically. The perfect recipe for some paranormal activity, don't you think?

During our visits to Rosehill, we have gotten some EVPs; however, one of the more convincing pieces of potential evidence was captured one evening when we decided to incorporate the use of dowsing rods or, as some prefer the term, divining rods. Now given the fact that there is a small pond located at the lowermost section in the cemetery, it would seem likely we would receive false readings or motion simply because dowsing rods were originally intended as a type of divination employed in attempts to locate groundwater, buried metals or ores, gemstones, oil, gravesites, and many other objects and materials; even though, we still believed that it was worth the attempt. One of our photographers took some photos of our group's leader standing in front of Lester Stillwell's grave using the rods. From time-to-time they would cross, other times the rods would remain pointing straight. When the photographs were later examined, in the images depicting the rods crossing, there appeared to be an orb lingering above the user's head.

Other experiences included the feeling of being watched, even in broad daylight. One experience was shared by several of our members. We were on top of one of the few mausoleums in the cemetery. Like I mentioned before, the cemetery has different levels of ground and, in this particular area, you can actually be virtually standing on the roof of the mausoleums. Usually an area above would register at a warmer temperature, but it registered much colder. On a return trip to Rosehill, in the spot we recalled, there was now a fresh burial. Was it a coincidence — or a prelude to an impending death?

Captain Kidd's treasure elm tree marker is located at the highest point in Rosehill Cemetery.

We also identified the type of tree, an Elm, mentioned many times in publications: Reportedly, the infamous Elm trees, better known as Kidd's Rangers, served as markers for Captain Kidd's buried treasure to guide Kidd back to his buried gold. Many famous pirates landed in Central New Jersey, including Blackbeard, who attacked farms and villages in Middletown. The "Morgan" section of Sayreville was named after Captain Morgan's descendants. The Raritan Bay was a haven for pirates back in the late 1600s and 1700s. Some of their shipmates settled in New Jersey, no doubt avoiding any prosecution back in England, and are buried in church graveyards in the area.

The Analysis

Because of the atmosphere, there are certain cemetery locations that can contribute to the contamination of potential evidence, which, even in the most ideal situation, can be difficult to gather. In our opinion, it is best to focus on a particular cemetery; gather as much evidence as you can by making repeated trips and take the time to sort through everything with extreme care, checking all the details.

We are not finished with Rosehill. While we have reviewed most of the EVP work, the jury is still out on a good part of it. What is disappointing, overall, is simply that the shark attacks happened so long ago, almost ninety-six years to be exact, so there is very little left to be able to view exactly how the situation was at the time of the attacks. The railroad trestle where Lester Stillwell's body was recovered from the water is now gone, as are most of the roads, footpaths, and docks leading to the creek. The drawbridge where the first sighting of the shark by Captain Cottrell took place was replaced many years ago and the geography of the land has changed over time, giving way to progress. All that remains, barely, is the Matawan Creek. The only reminder of Lester Stillwell is Stillwell's repair garage that undoubtedly remains a part of the Stillwell family. Nonetheless, the history is amazing.

As we stated in the beginning of this story, there was a "Great White" that had been caught; however, it was never determined, beyond doubt, that this, in fact, was the one that mauled twelve-year-old Joseph Dunn or that killed Lester Stillwell, so once again folklore enters and the story remains.

Gravesite of Captain Thomas V. Cottrell, deemed as one of the heroes of the shark attack incident. Site is in Rosehill Cemetery.

Chapter 5

Murder at the Matawan Mansion

The Burrowes Mansion in Matawan was built in 1723 and occupied by John Burrowes, known as the "Corn King," just a few short years later. Burrowes was a family man with a wife, a son, and four daughters. He was by trade a merchant of grains and produce, shipping these products back and forth to New York City. His wife and children helped him since the granaries were situated to the rear of the mansion.

The Burrowes family had strong ties to the Revolutionary War as John's only son, also named John, was one of the organizers who formed the first New Jersey Company. The company's first muster was held in the mansion's garden shortly before the company headed to Long Island to join up with more of General George Washington's men. The Battle at Monmouth was upon New Jersey and, because the elder John was very successful with his business, corn became in large demand during the war. Neighbors frequently stole grain, which made the Burrowes family a target.

Now the Burrowes Mansion is not without tragedy. One fateful night in June, the younger John Burrowes, who became a Major during the war, was a target of spies planted by the British and British rebels from Long Island. They had gotten word that Burrowes would be visiting his home and they wanted to capture him, so on this fateful night the Burrowes Mansion's front door was kicked in, but not before Major Burrowes was able to escape through one of the back windows, leaving his family to fend for themselves. During the break-in, a confrontation ensued and a British soldier was shot and killed. Another British soldier demanded that Major Burrowe's wife relinquish the shawl she was wearing so it could be used to dress the wounded soldier's injury and, when she refused, the soldier stabbed her to death!

Angered that Major Burrowes had escaped and how defiant his wife was (or that she really didn't suffer as much as they would have liked her to), the British ransacked the mansion and the granaries were set afire. Surprisingly enough, the mansion came through unscathed. However, the elder Burrowes was taken prisoner, as a sort of consolation prize, only to be released after a few months.

Burrowes Mansion in Matawan, New Jersey.

Bloodstains mark the spot where the Major's wife met her gruesome death as she came down the stairs. Does her spirit linger in this miracle mansion? Does the Major's spirit return only to find his wife dead on the stairs? Well, you be the judge. Summertime visitors are intrigued by the story; however, some of the locals refuse to even linger near the Mansion, no less enter. And at nightfall… Well, that is another story in itself!

As folklore tales go, emanating from the nearby town of Freehold is that of a local girl who married her longtime love, a soldier, in her father's apple orchard. This was common practice with many young couples staring war in the face, and this was also true of the elder John Burrowes' family. The soldier left to go to war promising to return when the fruit was ripe. Unfortunately, during the Battle at Monmouth, he was killed and carried home by his fellow comrades through the apple orchard. It is said that his blood stained the apple trees and from then on whenever the apples grew, they grew with red circles on them. The locals called these apples "Monmouth Reds."

Chapter 6

The Cloaking

Where the Paranormal Ends and the Supernatural Begins

Stories, stories, stories... We simply had to find out for ourselves! Unfortunately, we cannot reveal the location; however, we did follow-up and were granted permission to see if what we had been hearing from some of the locals was, at least in part, true or had the story generated into its being out of control.

It is not unusual to hear from a business claiming they experience unexplained occurrences. This well-known chain of floral emporiums did just that. The manager of this specific location explained that at times they would hear a little girl making herself at home in the shop by playing with bells and other ornaments used by employees to create various holiday arrangements and other decorative items. They would hear her laughter and they would even leave out crayons and paper, toys and candy, and encourage who they believed to be this little girl to feel welcome. However, not every employee was comfortable with this, but then who really would be; someone who you cannot see? It goes against an older generation's saying, "Children should be seen and not heard." Places where you may not necessarily know a lot of the history may sometimes produce the most unusual and unexpected type of results. This place was in full bloom.

The Investigation

We arrived shortly before sundown and began setting up equipment. The shop was small, but had a basement and this was where the employees would place the objects for the little girl. The basement was primarily used for seasonal supplies, containers, and other supplies needed to make flower arrangements, as well as a large walk-in refrigerator to hold the overflow of finished arrangements of fresh flowers during peak holidays. There were a few aisles of metal shelving, but other than that it was fairly open and uncluttered. A small room off to the side for water meters and telephone equipment pretty much completed the floor plan.

As is common practice for NJGO, we had one of our psychics with us. What had transpired during the investigation was simply astonishing and after setting up the cameras and recorder we decided that in this situation it would be best to leave the building to see what would happen when no one was present. Could we entice the spirit of the little girl enough to hopefully capture her image on video or possibly the sound of her voice on our voice recorders? When we returned a short time later, guarding the building to make sure no one entered the area using motion sensors, the motion sensors sounded, but no one human, no one tangible, had entered. What we discovered upon re-entering the basement was the video cameras were turned off, but never lost time as if the cameras rolled the entire time we were absent. Did something or someone not want us to see? Was it the little girl just being a curious kid? We didn't really know what to think.

We asked the psychic what her impressions were about the basement. What was she seeing and feeling? She described a man in painter-type pants, a handyman of sorts. He told her that he was passing through the area and needed work. He was not from this area and would likely eventually move on. This is common no matter what century — 1700s, 1800s, or even present day. For now, though, he was attached to this building, the area, or the property on which this building rests. The psychic's impression was neither good nor bad. The other impression was she never "saw" the little girl. However, what she did see was a man. He wore a dark cloak and oddly enough he had his arm up, his cloak raised, and apparently he was protecting or shielding the little girl. Was he shielding her from us or something more? Was it the stranger with the painter's pants? The investigation continues.

Over on the far wall, opposite the room where the water meters and telephone equipment are, some members are photographing. The psychic is drawn to the area because she is picking up on something. She says something is there, but she can't quite put her finger on it yet. I asked her if she could draw on paper what she's seeing. What she draws is almost like the head of a shark. Further down that wall another member and I are sitting in a couple of chairs. All of a sudden the temperature in the room starts feeling a little cooler. As the psychic is following whatever this shark head is, she is now in our corner. Simultaneously the other member and myself are feeling extreme coldness starting to wrap around first each of our shoulders and then our thighs. As the other members catch up to the psychic and are now all in this area where we are sitting, you would think the temperature would start to rise. It didn't. What started happening next not only took us completely by surprise, but the shop manager and employee as well — the walk-in refrigerator started making noise as if it was going to get up and walk across the floor! Yet, the refrigerator was not even plugged in! In the room where the water meters and telephone equipment are, you could hear the modem start dialing up! It seemed as though all hell broke loose...but then it stopped and everything went silent.

The Analysis

In the days that followed, we reviewed the audio, video, and camera evidence from the investigation. Most of the video was nothing. The audio was nothing except for apparently the gate to hell that unleashed that night, but it was what we saw in the photographs that were surprising. The photos were taken in the area where the psychic knew something, sensed something was there, but couldn't put her finger on it, and drew on paper the image of a shark-like head. In one of the photos was an orb; in the orb was the image of a shark-like head…exactly what she had drawn on paper days before.

Through speaking with colleagues in the field and with our group being familiar with different types of hauntings, we determined that what we had experienced and encountered was an inhuman entity. An inhuman entity was never human. It is not something that you can control and they can be potentially dangerous. Upon further examination of photos taken that night, in some of the images, wherever an orb was captured on film, there was a smaller orb right beside it. This evidence was supported by the psychic's impressions or, better yet, the psychic's impressions were supported by evidence.

Was this cloaked spirit protecting the little girl from this inhuman spirit? Was the spirit in the painter's pants a temporary disguise of the inhuman entity thinking it would gain our trust? Any one of these assumptions is very plausible. We also found out that a long time ago up on the corner a short distance away, a little girl was struck and killed by a horse and carriage. We guess she hangs around to smell the flowers.

Inhuman Spirits

To give you a short understanding of inhuman spirits, these entities have never been human. They exist as an entity of their own. Inhuman spirits are able to manifest themselves in any form they choose, but generally manifest as a half-man and half-animal. Signs of inhuman spirits are a ferocious growl or other frightening sounds that appear to be coming from all directions. The air in the haunted area may appear heavy, much like dense fog, and the temperature will change drastically.

Prayer

"I call upon thee for your protection and help.
Today, tonight and forever more.
I place myself in your presence, to be surrounded by white light.
Guide me now to protect myself and help all those in need.
Keep me safe and warm until in death I sleep."

Gravesite of Mary Ellis.

Chapter 7

The Saga of Mary Ellis

Strange as this may first seem, along a stretch of U.S. Highway 1 southbound, just south of the Raritan River Bridge, is the gravesite of Sailor's Girl, located in the parking lot on a stone mound surrounded by a wrought iron fence behind the AMC Loews multiplex. This location was once home to the U.S. Highway 1 flea market. It is not what is in the movie theater that is interesting, but what people have seen from time to time outside in the parking lot. After all, why would there be a headstone and small graveyard in the parking lot near the river? When I visited here recently, the parking lot behind the theater complex was completely void of automobiles and I could not help but marvel at this huge structure as it came into view. The gravesite was nothing like I remembered from when the U.S. Highway 1 flea market occupied this same location — back then it was a simple mound with the wrought iron fence and a headstone.

Back in the days when sailing ships could go up and down the Raritan River, Mary Ellis (1750-1827), who was a spinster living in New Brunswick, had fallen in love with a sailor, a sea captain, and it is her grave that now sits rising about six feet above the surface of the parking lot. History allegedly has it that this sea captain who vowed to return to marry her seduced her. Unfortunately she waited and waited, but he never did return and it is said that each day Mary would ride her horse to the spot where her grave now stands hoping one day to see his ship sailing up the Raritan and coming home to her.

The song "Brandy" by the New Jersey band Looking Glass is said to have been inspired by the Mary Ellis story. The lyrics include the lines: "Brandy, you're a fine girl. What a good wife you would be. But my life, my lover, my lady is the sea." Mary's family home eventually became the site for the Route 1 Flea Market and later the Lowe's Theater complex. Now just to spice up this story a little, when Mary died, her family, who owned the land, buried her near the River. The family has since sold the land, but always with the caveat that the little grave plot remains. It is rumored that she is buried with her horse that kept the long lonely vigil with her.

Some movie-goers say that they believe Mary's spirit still waits along that section on "The Banks of the Raritan" and that they may have caught a glimpse of her, especially around sunset, on their way for their evening's entertainment. While others pass on this tale, it may be well to take note. Perhaps, before you settle down for your show at the theater, you should visit Mary's gravesite to pay your respects.

Chapter 8

The Infamous Spy House

Port Monmouth's Haunted Revolutionary Treasure

Just let your imagination run wild when you visit this two-story clapboard house on the shore. Built in 1648, it is considered the oldest structure in New Jersey and, by all claims, the most haunted in the United States. Located on Belford Harbor in the Middletown/Port Monmouth area, it certainly lives up to its nickname "The Spy House." Thomas Seabrook of Westchester, New York, purchased the land, but never had the chance to move his family to New Jersey. He was killed in an Indian raid. The widow Seabrook remarried a man by the name of Thomas Whitlock and the original home was built. The home's actual name is the Whitlock-Seabrook House; after a larger addition was built on the house, it was named the Seabrook Homestead and turned into an Inn during the Revolutionary War. It soon became a meeting place for both the British troops and the Americans to spy on one another. It also became a hang-out for pirates, as underground tunnels that lead out to the beach were discovered in later centuries. Another owner, the Reverend William Wilson, took over ownership in the 1800s.

Many pirates, including Captain Morgan and his crew, did their dirty business at the Inn — capturing and killing prisoners of other ships' crews, women, and children and holding them captive in leg irons in the Inn's dirt basement — are just some of the intrigue of this shore house. There have also been stories of many a death in the families associated with ownership of the home.

Infamous Spy House in Leonardo, New Jersey.

Claims that have been reported over the years include visitors to the property seeing a stern-looking sea captain in uniform peering through a telescope from a back upper window and the spirit of a young woman named Abigail, who perpetually awaits her husband's return from the sea. People also claim to hear her sobs and see her in the window of an upper floor bedroom. Some have also said they hear the sounds of a horse-drawn carriage approaching the house and of children playing.

On some of our visits to the Spy House we noticed a bullet hole in the old brass chandelier and mostly the feeling of anxiousness. Photos in past years have produced a shadowy image in a second floor window. With a house so rich with history and intrigue, it is a place you will just have to experience for yourself.

Much folklore surrounds this interesting structure located in Leonardo, New Jersey, on what was once a lightly traveled road, that has become known as the infamous Spy House. Set back between the road and a stretch of beach, the first section was built in 1648, with two additions constructed at later dates. Prior to it being temporarily closed for renovation, it was alleged to host, at the very least, twenty plus spirits; however, not all of its past inhabitants are present at one time, but you can be certain to run into a few, in various forums, at each visit. So come prepared.

The house has open views to Sandy Hook and New York City. The local name, Spy House, alludes to the intelligence war waged here by American patriots and their British and Loyalist adversaries who maintained a stronghold in New York. Legends that Americans used the house to monitor British ship movements are spiced with stories of pirates, underground tunnels, and a host of ghosts, starting with Thomas Whitlock, the first settler here in 1663.

This house was a tavern during Washington's day. The owner would put the welcome mat out to British troops, listen to what they were planning, and then pass the information onto Washington's men...hence the name "Spy House." This was before the pirates, who supposedly hid treasure near the house and stored their dead in the basement, used it. There are tunnels under the house and there have been ghosts seen of both a pirate and a child who died in the upstairs room. Soldiers were murdered there also, so with all this history the Spy House has been described as the "Grand Central Station of Ghosts" in New Jersey.

Captain Morgan House.

Folklore, Myths, or Legends of the Spy House

Folklore indicates that a visitor to the Spy House was looking for her child and saw a woman in period clothing hanging draperies. When the visitor spoke to the woman, there was no reply.

Near the fireplace in the main room were two captains' chairs and, when the spirit of a sea captain is present, the chair he is sitting on has a definite change in temperature from that of the other, feeling extremely cold to the touch. I personally experienced this temperature phenomenon on a visit many years ago.

Another story claims that a father and son were standing near the parking lot at the rear of the house, facing the water. Now, it is not uncommon to see individuals fishing at the far side of the parking lot, but, as the father and son stood there watching, they noticed one of the fishermen walking towards them, seemingly going to his car. As the fisherman walked along, he began to pass through several of the cars — as if he was walking a path that no longer existed. As it got closer, the apparition became more visibly transparent and then disappeared completely.

A bit more bazaar is the story of a 'nasty' sea captain who occasionally sits in the back windowed room of the second floor. Running almost the entire length of the house, the room faces the water and New York City, which was a stronghold of the British Army during the Revolutionary War. On occasion, he is known to bother visitors.

There is also the voice of a child, believed to be a young boy, coming from the top of what once was a staircase but has since been encased in the wall. Many other spirits come and go at various times, so when you visit the Spy House you never know who or what will make its presence known. The downstairs fireplace in the main room seems to be a portal that the spirits make good use of on their journey between realms.

One of the most intriguing accounts to come forth is that of a young lady walking down the front path from the house as a horse-drawn carriage pulls up in front. The young lady gets into the carriage and, as it begins its journey down the street, it seems to disappear into thin air. It would be a true experience to spend a night in the house; I most certainly would like to, as I am certain that most of you would too, if for the very least to discover the truth, folklore, legend, or myth? Well, we did just that!

The Investigation

It was just after the sun had begun to set when NJGO's team of paranormal investigators approached the Spy House. They immediately experienced the ominous feeling that they were being watched, a common sensation that most people feel when daring to visit here after-hours, but, unfortunately, the building is closed for renovations. I should preface what I just said with the main reason that the group was there that particular evening: It was their annual function that they call "Dining with the Ghosts." This may seem to some as being unusual, as most often the affair is held at an outdoor location, complete with candelabra and, hopefully, to encounter something. At the rear of the building is a small picnic area with benches and tables and, after eating, they decided that since the building was closed they would simply walk around and take a few photographs of the outside and possibly through some of the windows. As luck would have it, a park ranger had come to lower the American Flag for the evening and, interested in what we were doing, allowed us access to the building for a brief time while he was there.

The locals cannot resist retelling tales connected to the Spy House. One can just imagine the many stories that have been told throughout the years, with slight twists added here and there: from twenty-two spirits making their presence in the house known, you may encounter a few, possibly different ones, each time that you pay a visit. Who knows, you may even come away with your own version of the story!

View of Spy House from beach area.

General view of Port Monmouth's stretch of beach area.

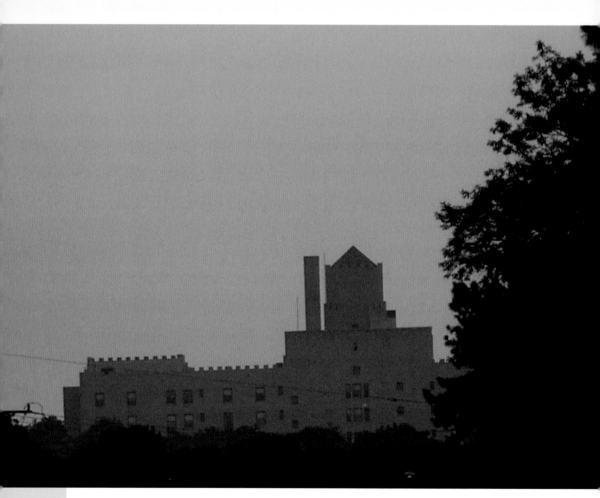

Haunting view of the former Royal Pines Hotel from the "Mob" and prohibition era.

Chapter 9

The Woman in White

Mob Ties to New Jersey

Berkeley Township is located in Ocean County and was incorporated as a township by an Act of the New Jersey Legislature on March 31, 1875. It began with an Army officer named Lt. Edward Farrow, who bought up the woodland with the idea of building a retirement community for former Army and Navy officers. He built a railroad station, shops, and even a resort hotel called the Royal Pines, but only eleven people ever built houses in what Farrow called Barnegat Park. Eventually he went bankrupt.

In the 1920s, Benjamin Sangor purchased the area. The New York and Miami developer imagined a vast and luxurious resort town catering to wealthy urban vacationers. Between 1928 and 1929, about 8,000 lots were sold in what was called "Pinewald," a "new-type of residential and recreational city-of-the-sea-and-pines." The area was to host a golf course, recreation facilities, and estate homes. The developers immediately began construction of the Pinewald pavilion and pier at the end of Butler Avenue.

The Royal Pines Hotel was a $1.1 million-dollar investment facing Crystal Lake. It was built on the site of an earlier hotel dating back to the days of Barnegat Park and was the focal point of the new community. The hotel was also used as an asylum and then later as a nursing home while changing ownerships. Mystery surrounds the former hotel that the Russian architect W. Oltar-Jevsky constructed in the early 1920s. Al Capone is said to have frequented its halls and perhaps even venturing beneath the structure to the lake in tunnels that were especially designed for smuggling alcohol during the Prohibition. It has been rumored that in the 1930s the then Royal Pines Hotel was frequented by society's elite who for $1.90 a drink consumed prohibition liquor under the watchful eye of men who had guns strapped under their coats. Should this be fact or has the truth since passed into the annals of time.

If you have ever traveled the Garden State Parkway, once you reach the Berkeley Township (Bayville) area, in the distance, you will get a glimpse of a large pinkish building that is commonly referred to as Al Capone's Hotel (should you be traveling south glance to your left or if traveling north glance to your right). If you are in the area of the Central Regional High School, the structure can easily be seen and is only a stone's throw from there.

While a resident of Berkeley Township, I ventured to this location several times, though I was never able to gain entrance to investigate. Due to the nature of the current use of the building as a nursing home, the owners were reluctant, not wishing the residents to be disturbed or possibly frightened, which is certainly understandable. Just walking the grounds, an eerie feeling overcomes you and you can, perhaps, picture the activity that once had taken place here during the heyday of prohibition. When standing on the shoreline of beautiful Crystal Lake, simply let your thoughts wander for a moment and you will be able to picture the many canoes and rowboats, the women in long, full dresses holding parasols and being paddled about by their male escorts wearing spats and vests (the clothing of the time) or simply strolling along the banks of what was once a highly traveled to hotel and lake resort.

If you plan to be there at sunset, I would suggest that you park your car in the parking lot and close to the entrance road as street parking is prohibited. From this point, you can take some interesting photographs and walk to the far side of the lake, where you will have a full view of the building — you never know what may appear. You may get a glimpse of those bygone days of the mob or overhear a conversation…one that you were not intended to hear.

Chapter 10

Whispers on the Ocean Breeze

Legends of Asbury Park

I recall as a young boy making frequent visits to Asbury Park with my parents and again later in the 1950s and 1960s with my own children. What a great place to spend the day — a beach resort complete with boardwalk, amusements, rides, and plenty of good places to eat. What more could a kid ask for except for possibly a ghost or two? At the time I was not aware of the paranormal or all that it entailed.

This vacant palace arcade and the famous Tillie the Clown still greet visitors to Asbury's boardwalk.

In its heyday, during the early part of the twentieth century, Asbury Park was host to men in derby hats and women with long dresses carrying parasols walking the boards and basket-type conveyances that carryied those who became tired from walking the length of the boardwalk and wanted to ride back, being pushed helter-skelter along the boards. These conveyances still existed during my time; I can picture them in my mind, hearing the rumbling of the wheels as they hit the separations between the boards. The stretch of beach being crowded had never changed from the early times to my visits there. Toward the latter part of the twentieth century, Asbury Park gradually became a "Ghost Town" — the amusements disappeared along with most of the businesses. Deteriorating buildings were being boarded up with very few frequenting the area. The once active strip of beach was empty and eerie feelings would overcome those who did venture there.

During the twentieth century, however, Asbury Park was firmly established among New Jersey's foremost seashore resorts, vying with Cape May, Atlantic City, and nearby Long Branch for visitors. It sparkled with the presence of five-and-dime czar Frank W. Woolworth; jazz great Duke Ellington; adventure-travel writer Lowell Thomas; New York City mayor Ed Koch; band leader Arthur Pryor, whose composition "Whistler and His Dog" became the theme song for TV's *Leave It to Beaver*; Olympic track hopeful Frank Budd; actors Bud Abbott, Danny DeVito, and Jack Nicholson; Big Band trumpeter Harry James; actor and civil rights crusader Canada Lee; award-winning poet Margaret Widdemer; NAACP founder W.E.B. DuBois; crooner Frank Sinatra; and teacher Elizabeth Gray Vining, whose autobiography was turned into *The King and I*.

There is a leering clown face that is a vivid reminder of the boardwalk's past glory. Bruce Springsteen fans are hoping that someone will rescue the mural and Clown Face on the side of the old Palace amusement arcade, as Bruce once posed with Tillie the Clown in a promo photo. The arcade has been slated for destruction since part of its interior collapsed some time ago and the Palace once contained two great spook rides, an elaborate funhouse, and a huge ferris wheel that extended upward through an opening in the roof. Today the Asbury Park oceanfront is a bleak no-man's land of closed businesses and stymied development dreams. Bruce Springsteen still lives nearby — when you least expect him, he will show up at the Stone Pony Club to treat the guests to a performance.

Are spirits of days passed still walking the boards, frolicking on the sandy stretch of beach, or standing by a vacant eatery? Is the smell of hotdogs, popcorn, and cotton candy permeating the air? Are they riding a now non-existent amusement ride? Can you still here the eerie sounds of the carnival-like music being played as you walk the boards? Some of the nearby residents claim that you may even hear the music of the famous carousel building from days gone by, even though the carousel is long gone. However, I am happy to say that Asbury Park is on an upward trend and trying to regain its former atmosphere as a resort area. I am certain the spirits appreciate it; I know that I do.

View of Asbury Park's deserted carousel building.

Located in this New Jersey shore town of Asbury Park, the Stone Pony is a pilgrimage for Rock and Roll fans worldwide and one of the most widely known music venues. Its former occupants include a restaurant called Mrs. Jay's and a deserted disco called the Magic Touch. Jack Roig and Butch Pielka, who had been working in a club at the Seaside Heights boardwalk, a more southerly resort area, founded the Stone Pony on February 9, 1974.

Two years later, the Jersey band Southside Johnny and the Asbury Jukes, the house-band for the Pony for much more of the seventies, debuted their first album during a live radio broadcast from the Stone Pony. The Jukes are known for their rendition of Sam Cooke's "Havin A Party," which became the unofficial theme song not only for the Pony, but also of Asbury Park. Before he became famous, Bruce Springsteen, and many other bands, made appearances at the Pony; some were even discovered there, including the recently deceased saxophonist Clarence Clemons and the Red Bank Rockers. Clemons eventually became one of the founders of Springsteen's E Street Band and, in 1972, Clemons became Springsteen's legendary side man or the "Big Man," as he was lovingly nicknamed.

Sadly, the E Street Band's saxophone player passed on, June 18, 2011, from stroke complications at the age of only sixty-nine. Having deep roots at the Jersey Shore, it leaves little doubt that his legendary sax solo from Springsteen's 1975 hit song "Jungleland" will be heard in Asbury Park for decades to come. Some folks even say that on a quiet moonlit summer night the song can faintly be heard drifting on the ocean breeze as you pass near the Stone Pony.

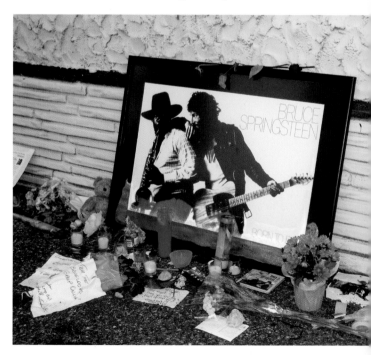

Recently deceased, Clarence Clemon's memorial is located outside the legendary Stone Pony Club.

Legendary Stone Pony Club, just a short walk from Asbury's boardwalk.

Who's Really Sitting Next to You?

The Paramount Theatre shares space with the Asbury Park Convention Hall on the boardwalk along the Atlantic Ocean, where an arcade spans the boardwalk. It is bordered by the ocean on the east and Bradley Park on the west connects the two. It is rumored that this landmark theater is home to some strange happenings.

In 1939, the famous Asbury Park's Paramount Theater caught fire, specifically the fourth floor, resulting in the deaths of four showgirls. Upon entering the theater, many curiosity seekers have reported that as you ascend your way to the upper floors, you feel as though you are being followed, the air seems to thicken and a feeling of oppression overcomes you. The building also seems to have electricity even when there was no power source. Were there still scheduled performances? Do these suddenly departed showgirls still perform at the Paramount Theater? No one really knows for sure; however, you may should you ever pay a visit there!

View of the legendary Paramount Theater connected to the Asbury Park Convention Hall.

Old 'Haunts' Never Die

The Stephen Crane House is located on Fourth Street in Asbury Park. Stephen Crane was most famous for penning the book *The Red Badge of Courage*. Both Crane and Asbury Park emerged on this earth in 1871 and the Crane House was built in 1878, originally named the Arbutus Cottage. Crane cherished his time in Asbury Park; he attended public schools here and spent every summer as a teen in Asbury Park. He wrote articles and features for newspapers and eventually wrote several books after furthering his education elsewhere. After his untimely death in England in 1900, his widow and their three youngest children moved to Asbury Park. He was born in Hillside, New Jersey, and buried there, in Evergreen Cemetery, not far from the old brick rectory, in which he was born and near where I once lived with my family. Crane was only twenty-eight years of age at the time of his passing specifically on June 5, 1900. Does the spirit of Stephen Crane still walk the streets of Asbury Park each summer?

Where the Past Becomes Present

Book-ending Asbury Park's boardwalk is two pavilions. The southern, non-renovated building is called "The Casino Arcade." By walking through to the opposite side from the Asbury side you will enter the Ocean Grove boardwalk; however, at certain times there may be one slight difference — or so say the locals. When certain conditions prevail, you may have the distinct feeling that you are the only one there and have taken a step back in time. Today, it is said that the surroundings may appear to be a bit distorted and the sounds of the old carousel can be faintly heard even though it has long been removed.

My father and mother recalled many times of going to the Asbury Park boardwalk since they were young adults back in the 1920s and this story, except for the hearing of the carousel, had been told many times when the family gathered and were discussing the 'old days' at Asbury, so I would not be too quick in discounting what some of the locals are talking about today.

World War II U-boats and German Sailors

Stories dating back to the Second World War have spawned much speculation and folklore; however, one story may possibly go down in the annals of history as being factual…

On some secluded stretches of beach you may hear voices, whispering in German, of submarine sailors who casually came ashore during the wee hours of the morning on many a non-moonlit night during the Second World War?

View of Asbury's famous Convention Hall.

Elaborating a bit on the "submarine" scenario, the father of a high school friend of our family's, during the World War II years, was a member of the German-American Bund that was located in New Jersey. A part of his obligations as a member was that once each month he and a few other members would head towards a pre-designated location on a lonely stretch of sand at Asbury Park, or in very close proximity, sometime after the hour of midnight. Legend claims that this stealth operation was to meet a German submarine at a specific time and help with the inflatable raft from the sub that would come ashore under the cloak of darkness, bringing with it a few of the submarine's crew. This gave them the opportunity to spend the next day or two lounging on the warm sunny beaches at Asbury Park intermingling with the American civilian population that flocked to the resort during the summer months. Also coming ashore each time were one or two non-crewmembers who would not be returning — they were usually here for clandestine operations, spying, or other unknown reasons!

Allegedly, and as difficult as it may be to believe, this operation was never discovered. It continued almost until the war was over. Area residents never really knew just how vulnerable our coastline was to infiltration during this wartime period. Of course, there is an easy way to find out for yourself — you will just have to go there! Maybe you will experience the paranormal firsthand or be privy to a residual haunting of those long but really not forgotten days. Who knows? A spirit or two may wander back to a more peaceful time.

As a young boy in the 1940s, I vividly recall on one trip that my parents and I made to Asbury Park an instance when many of the visitors on the boardwalk near convention hall rushed to view what appeared to be a ship exploding about a mile out in the ocean. Flames and smoke could be seen and the excitement was overwhelming. At that time, I did not realize what had actually taken place, not until many years after the Second World War had ended.

Much progress is being made to restore this beautiful area to its once magnificent state and it is beginning to flourish once again as the shore resort that it once was. One visit there will most certainly convince you of this, so please do not miss this opportunity when in Asbury.

For the not too faint at heart, staying alone too long after sunset may prove to be an experience that you will not soon forget. However, if you do plan on visiting Asbury Park, do not forget to bring along your camera and a digital voice recorder, as some of those long-ago, uninvited wartime visitors may pose for you or implant a message on your recorder — that is, if you respect them and speak to them nicely. This is also provided that folklore can be photographed and recorded! If you can speak German, it may be to your advantage!

Must-See Places

The Paranormal Museum, located next to the Paranormal Book Store in Asbury Park, is the only one of its kind in New Jersey. The uniqueness surpasses any expectations we had from our first visit to the many subsequent visits that continue today. The museum, and the manner in which it provides complete curiosity to both non-believers and believers, has a place in Jersey history. The legend of the Jersey Devil is important not only to pass down from generation to generation, but also because so many hundreds of people lay claim to have actually seen this devil child, especially at the Jersey Shore and the Pine Barrens, which is unique to New Jersey in itself.

Another unique place in preserving New Jersey Folklore is located on the boardwalk of Atlantic City. While it is considered an attraction, it is the only one of its kind as well. Haunted Attractions is a place you can experience the legends of both the Jersey Devil and the legends of the Jersey Coast Pirates in a full, very realistic animated environment. You don't see many places like these and they are a great little departure from all the state-trotting we do.

Paranormal Book Store and Museum…
where you and the bizarre meet, located in
Asbury Park's business district.

Chapter 11

Voices from the Past

The Hindenburg LZ-129 Crash Site

Historic events easily foster the birth of folklore, as it has been alleged that, especially on summer evenings during thunderstorm activity, many unusual happenings are said to take place in the vicinity of the Hindenburg crash. The area of Hangar No.1 is also reported by many who visit the site to be haunted.

As fate would have it, a gentleman, with several of his friends, from Columbus Jersey, made an eleventh hour decision to travel to Lakehurst, New Jersey, to be on hand for the scheduled arrival of the Giant Airship LZ129 Hindenburg at 7:25 p.m. the evening of May 6, 1937. Barely arriving on time, seeing the giant airship already visible in the stormy sky over Lakehurst, the men rushed to where most of the spectators were gathered, working their way through the crowd. Chaos began as the night sky turned red and people began running from the tremendous flash of the explosion — the Hindenburg was being consumed by flames and the aluminum structure was beginning to crumble under the tremendous heat being generated. Soon, the giant of the sky crashed to the ground.

Marker located at the Hindenburg crash site.

A slightly charred piece of the Hindenburg's skin (outer covering).

During the ensuing chaos, tiny pieces of the "skin" (outer covering) of the airship fluttered to the ground, one piece landing near where the gentleman from Columbus was standing. Still on fire, he immediately stepped on it to extinguish the fast-burning flame, as he wanted it as a remembrance of the scene he had just witnessed. Arriving, back home, he thought it a good idea to cut the postcard size piece into slivers, one for himself and a piece for each of his friends. One of those slivers now resides in my archive.

Every year on the anniversary of the disaster, individuals who gather at the crash site cannot help but to come away from it saying that while they were there, they had a strange feeling of not being alone. It seems that some visitors from the past are still there or simply come back to pay their 'spirited' respects!

Psychic Reactions

Holding the tiny piece of outer skin in her cupped hands, NJGO's psychic's first reaction was startling. "My hands felt hot, very hot! A woman's face briefly flashed before me and I can hear sounds of screaming, of running, and a great deal of terror. Very distinct is a voice shouting out the words 'Away the Lines.' I can see the letters HIN and I'm being directed to the top right portion where a fire that is engulfing what appears to be a flying ship began. This is where this piece originated." Not known previously to me was the location on the giant airship from which the piece had originated. Since this evaluation I have made several visits to Lakehurst and its infamous haunted Hangar No. 1.

Extremely haunted is the tarmac area in front of the famous Hangar No. 1 and inside the hangar at the NAS (Naval Air Station) at Lakehurst, New Jersey. Voices have been heard revealing the mass confusion related to the disaster of that infamous evening, when thirty-six unsuspecting individuals, returning from an air voyage to Germany, lost their lives in a ball of flame in a matter of only a few seconds. From inside the hangar, at times when no one should be present, the whirring of engines can be heard. A lone, misty figure has been seen lingering high on one of the overhead catwalks, near the roof-line, and when called to, there is no reply. On some evenings, near one of the security lights inside the hangar, what appears to be a figure can be seen, but when security personnel move towards it for a closer look…the figure seems to have vanished!

I discussed this with another of NJGO's psychics and I was informed that when she had the opportunity to visit this area many years before visitors were actually permitted to visit a small building to the right of the crash site (when viewing it from the tarmac in front of Hanger No. 1) that was used for the actual temporary morgue. Initially, there may have been some bodies of the crash victims brought directly into the hangar, but soon after taken to the smaller building. Some of the victims were immediately transported to area hospitals; thirty-six people had perished in this horrific accident so it is not surprising that stories emanate of spirits that still haunt the tarmac and the hanger that once housed this magnificent giant of the sky.

Exterior and interior views of the
infamous "Haunted" Hanger No.1.

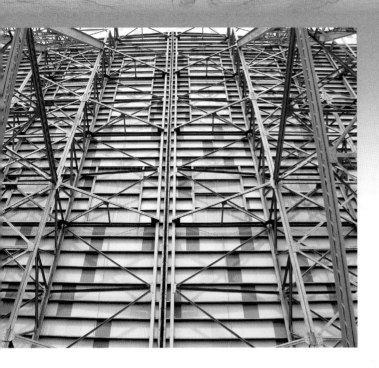

Chapter 12

Ghostly Ships along the Jersey Shore

Captain Sandovate

When Captain Don Sandovate voyaged from Spain to the New World in search of treasure, he found gold in abundance. However, among his crew there were many sailors who did not wish to share the newfound wealth with the monarchs of Spain. On their journey up the Atlantic Coast, the sailors mutinied and imprisoned their captain, tying him to the main mast and refusing to give him food or drink. Day after day, the captain lay exposed to the hot sun of summer, his body drying up as the treacherous sailors worked around him. Finally, his pride broken, Don Sandovate begged: "Water, please give me just one sip of water." The mutineers found this amusing, and started carrying water up the main mast and holding it just out of reach of their former captain. In the terrible heat of a dry summer, the captain did not survive long without water. A few days after the mutiny, the captain succumbed to heat and thirst. The new captain, a greedy Spaniard with no compassion in his soul, left Don Sandovate tied to the mast, his body withering away, while the ship turned pirate and plundered its way up the coast, but Providence was watching the ruthless men and a terrible storm arose and drove the ship deep into the Atlantic, where it remains with all her hands and the body of Don Sandovate still tied to the broken mast.

Shortly after the death of the mutineers-turned-pirates, an eerie ghost ship began appearing along the coast, usually in the calm just before a storm. It had the appearance of a Spanish treasure ship, but its mast was broken, its sails torn, and the corpse of a noble-looking Spaniard was tied to the mast. The ship was crewed by skeletons in ragged clothing. As it passed other ships or houses near the shore, the skeletons would stretch out bony hands and cry: "Water. Please. Give us just one sip of water." However, no one can help them, for they are eternally doomed to roam the Atlantic, suffering from thirst in payment for their terrible deeds against their captain and the good people living along the Atlantic Coast.

Pirate Ship. *Artwork by Frank Consoli.*

Today, many have seen this ghost ship with its mast broken, the captain's body tied to the main mast, and skeletons as the crew. Could this be legend turned folklore or fact? Possibly, when vacationing at the New Jersey Shore, you may experience this for yourself but do not blink as you may miss one!

The Protector

Captain John Paul Jones, originally from Scotland, was nicknamed "Father of the American Navy" during the Revolutionary War. Famous for the statement "I have not yet begun to fight," his status was sealed with his actions during the war — things that legends are made of.

In 1773, Jones, who was a successful merchant sailor involved in trade on the Atlantic Ocean between England, Africa, the West Indies, and America, defended himself in an attack by greedy sailors resulting in Jones killing a man. Believing he would not be tried fairly, he escaped to America and changed his name, adding the name Jones. He came to America at a time of heightened suppression from England's tax impositions and control, which resulted in the beginning of the American Revolution. Jones, being sympathetic to America's quest for liberty from England and how unfairly the people of his native Scotland suffered because of the British government, was quick to volunteer his services and expertise for the cause. His successes included capturing more than a dozen British ships in a single trip. This rattled the British government that the American army could reach them so easily. Jones's goal was to capture someone important and then negotiate for the release of American soldiers that were held in British jails. This was a bold move, but a little step that had huge results. Jones went on to do similar acts, earning him the title, according to the British, a pirate. Eventually an accidental explosion of a slow grenade resulting in the destruction of a British ship, Jones claimed a victory. It was a victory for America. Jones campaigned for a strong Navy, but the newly formed nation did not have the funds to support such a worthy service of protection. Eventually the Navy disbanded and Jones moved onto Russia and France and eventually was instrumental in his efforts to continue helping with the release of Americans imprisoned abroad. He died in France in 1792.

It remains a mystery why the American government made little effort to have Captain Jones returned to America and how important it would become for generations to come to celebrate and pay tribute to Jones's legendary patriotism as the war hero he was. It wasn't until Brigadier General Horace Porter, who served under Ulysses S. Grant during the Civil War, traced Jones back to Paris and his remains were located in a long-forgotten and built-over cemetery. It wasn't until 1905 that three lead coffins were dug up and identified Jones's very well preserved and embalmed remains. It would be discovered Jones died of kidney disease.

His body made the long and overdue trip, waiting over one hundred years to return where he belonged, the United States of America. His truly final resting place is in a crypt fit for a hero that lies underneath the chapel at the U.S. Naval Academy.

Is Captain John Paul Jones still protecting our Jersey coastlines in the afterlife? According to local folklore, on misty days you can still see the outline of his ship off the coast of New Jersey beaches, so do not be alarmed; after all, he is simply protecting you.

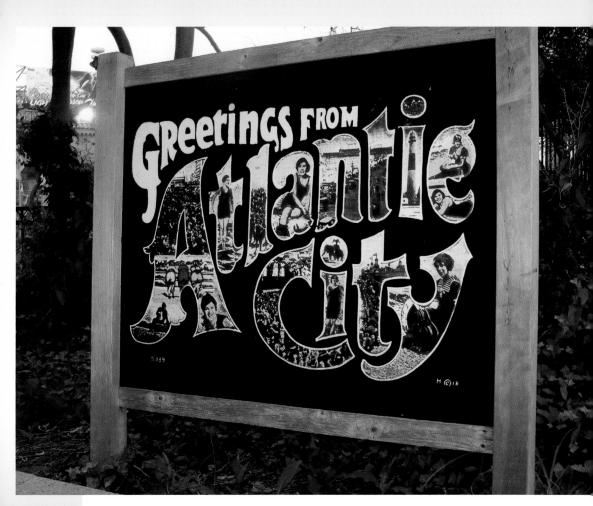

Sign greeting visitors to Atlantic City.

Chapter 13

Historic Legends of Atlantic City

All along the coast, New Jersey still boasts many huge Victorian-style houses mostly built for wealthy families from New York and Philadelphia that considered the Jersey Shore, and New Jersey for that matter, a premier vacation destination with New York a couple of hours away and Philadelphia just about an hour away.

Known nationally as a resort city for fine dining, shops, and gambling located in Atlantic County, the city was the inspiration for the board game "Monopoly." This southern New Jersey city hugs the Atlantic Ocean between islands and marshlands. Its eight miles of land became prime real estate and, in the mid-1850s, the Belle House was built, Atlantic City's first hotel. Railroad service began as well and was eventually renamed the Reading Railroad. Twenty years later the roads were also more accessible to reach the city, especially people from Philadelphia, Pennsylvania. The historic, massive seven-mile boardwalk was built in 1870, largely due to hotel owners complaining of the sand from the beach being dragged in on guests' feet. Many hotels and rooming houses were built by the end of the era, which brought wealthy tourists especially in the 1920s when the liquor flowed during prohibition and gambling was conducted in the back rooms of clubs, hotels, and restaurants. It also brought poverty, crime, and corruption.

The infamous Steeplechase Pier, more commonly known as the "Steel Pier," was built in 1882. It is directly across from what is now the Taj Mahal Casino. The pier's main draw was the diving horse and diving bell. A horse, rode on by a woman in a bathing suit (and bathing cap), slides down a steep sixty-foot slide into a large pool of water, much to the squealing delight of tourists. In the 1960s, tourists could huddle in a diving bell and be lowered into the ocean briefly. The original Steel Pier was destroyed by fire in 1982, but not before folks had the chance to see impressive performers like Charlie Chaplin, W. C. Fields, Bob Hope, Abbot and Costello, the legendary (and fellow New Jerseyan) Frank Sinatra, and the Rolling Stones. Many of the massive hotels were considered luxurious for the time period and many of them spanned several city blocks. On the start of a decline, many hotels were used for cheap apartments and nursing home facilities. It wasn't until the 1960s and '70s that many of these grand structures were demolished to make way for the casinos you see today. Only two of the original piers still exist. Many of the smaller hotels off the boardwalk managed to escape demolition. A hurricane in 1944 destroyed a small portion of the boardwalk and one pier.

General view of Atlantic City.

These impressive hotels of eras gone by no longer exist. The Belloe House was one of the oldest, built in 1853. The United States Hotel took up full city blocks between Atlantic, Pacific, Delaware, and Maryland Avenues. It must have been a sight to see. Most were finished being built in the early 1900s. The Marlborough House, built in 1903, is where Bally's Casino is now. The one that impresses us the most is the Traymore Hotel. It was built in 1879, but, unfortunately, it was demolished in 1972. These structures, compared to structures nowadays, looked like castles.

With all of this in mind it became clear — and peaked our interest as investigators — of the possibility of perhaps experiencing residual hauntings. With so much history, so much energy enveloping Atlantic City's eight miles, and so much activity (whether good or bad), it must be haunted, so we set out from time to time to check out specific locations where some of these bygone era structures once stood. We also decided to investigate to see if there was any folklore attached to Atlantic City.

There are indeed some stories attached to Atlantic City. Resorts Casino was the first casino built in our generation and it stands to reason that it has seen a lot of triumphs as well as tribulations for its guests. How about residents from time gone by? Perhaps. The Chalfonte House and the Haddon House sat in the vicinity of Resorts in 1868 and 1869 respectively. The Ambassador Hotel rested somewhere between what is now the Tropicana Casino and the Resorts Casino. During World War II, the Chalfonte House was used as a hospital of sorts. People have claimed to see glowing nurses, soldiers in wheelchairs, and children in carriages roaming the boardwalk. Soldiers walking the halls in the hotel registration area and in the parking lot have been said to be seen on several occasions. These "sightings" transcend over the years time and time again, including reports of seeing a spectral bride and groom inside the now Resorts Casino and very early in the morning a woman dressed in black feeding cats just below the boardwalk on the beach. Perhaps she's been feeding these cats since the 1800s. People have claimed she feeds cats from not only her dimension, but also from our dimension; they are said to see many cats congregating in that area, strange to say the least. Then again animals can see things that we cannot because of their heightened sixth sense. Examples like this are usually seen in the infrared and ultraviolet spectrums. With so many people's accounts, it has to be true.

Postcard photo view of the Traymore Hotel in its heyday and the destruction of the famous Atlantic City hotel.

Postcard photo view of the Traymore Hotel's destruction.

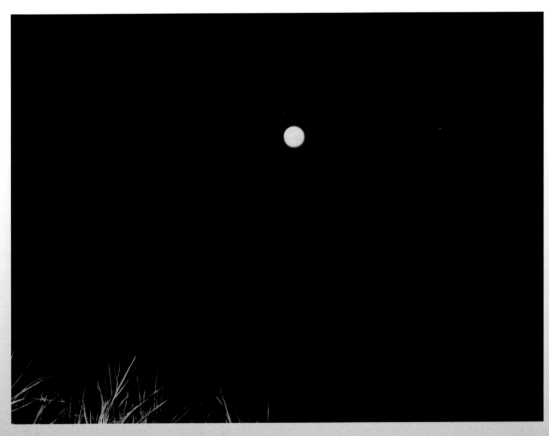

Hauntingly beautiful Atlantic City moonlit beach scene.

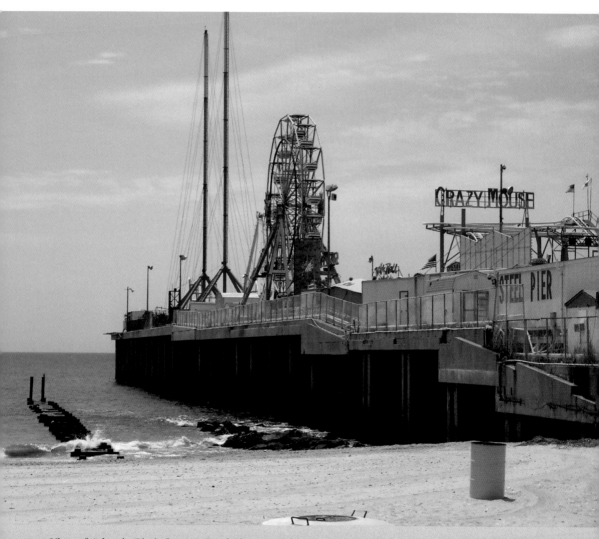

View of Atlantic City's famous Steel Pier.

Entrance to Atlantic City's famous Steel Pier.

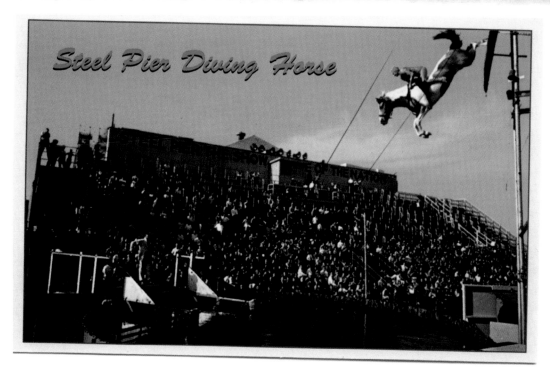

Postcard photo view of Atlantic City's legendary Diving Horse attraction.

Mobsters, Prohibition, & the Jersey Shore

It would be remiss to not include the spirit of bootlegging and mobsters who frequented Atlantic City and the surrounding shore areas. Presidents, dignitaries, celebrities, and gangsters frequented the place, staying at massive palaces like the United States Hotel, Ritz-Carlton, and the Ambassador Hotel. With the marshes and inlets that surround Atlantic City, it was a breeding ground to conduct illegal business for the New York, Philadelphia, and Chicago mobs, rich with European whiskey being imported. Atlantic City became sort of a neutral ground for these mobsters from around the country to converge for a little rest and relaxation too. The Ambassador Hotel was the site of a three-day National Convention for the mobs in 1929. Imagine back-alley gambling dens and speakeasies. For less than half a century, until gambling was eventually legalized in the late 1970s, this existed, but it all came with a price. The likes of Al Capone escaped a certain death during the convention, fled to Philadelphia by train, and spent some time in prison in Eastern State Penitentiary for a simple gun possession charge to avoid getting hit. Nicky Scarfo also escaped death. Because of his violent behavior and family connections, he was made the "capo" of Atlantic City. Eventually the end of an era, Atlantic City had turned into slums and Las Vegas became the entertainment capitol of the world. The mobs lost interest in Atlantic City and it wasn't until the spring of 1978 that Atlantic City was beginning to resurrect itself and eventually so did the mobs.

One of the many entranceways where Bootleggers transported
ashore their illegal "liquid booty" at Atlantic City.

There was killing going on all around the Atlantic City area, power
struggles within the mafia families, theft of whiskey shipments, and destitute
individuals who gambled their paychecks away. There's an odd energy in
Atlantic City. A lot has transpired over the decades, but you just can't put
your finger on it. Could the spirits of yesteryear affect the environment there
today? Will the future repeat the past? You decide.

Refuge for A Legend

When Capone arrived in Atlantic City for the National (Mobs) Convention
in 1929, he came fresh off the St. Valentine's Day Massacre and just days
before arriving in Atlantic City battered three of his soldiers for being disloyal
in his home turf of Chicago. He was out of control, brutal, stripped of most

of his power, and rivals were lining up to see him dead. When he made his hasty exit from the convention, heading on a train to Philadelphia, he was avoiding a certain death. When he arrived in Philadelphia, he handed himself over to the police on the mere charge of carrying a concealed weapon because he felt that being imprisoned would be safer than being on the streets.

Eastern State Penitentiary, just a stone's throw from Atlantic City, is known to be the sixth most haunted place in the United States. It was one of the most famous and expensive prisons in the world. It had running water before the White House in Washington, DC. The prison opened in 1829. When Capone arrived in the spring of 1929, he would be spending the next eight months in a cell. While he was incarcerated, he enjoyed many amenities other prisoners did not. His cell was lavishly decorated with fine furniture, fine artwork, and a radio, on which he listened to waltzes. In the few short months of his stay at Eastern State Penitentiary, it was rumored he saw ghosts of fellow gangster rivals and would talk to them as if they were having a conversation with him. He most likely was starting to lose his sense of reality. Records show he had his appendix removed and was being treated to baths to help with syphilis that he contracted during his travels.

New Jersey Ghost Organization's travels led us to Eastern State Penitentiary several years ago. While the penitentiary is now closed and has been mostly abandoned since the early 1970s, with its empty cell blocks, crumbling walls, and long empty guard towers, you can still feel thousands of eyes are watching. The prison is massive with its wagon wheel floor plan and spans eleven acres.

Al Capone's "luxury" cell at Eastern State Prison.

Interior cellblock view at Eastern State Prison.

Chapter 14

Sandy Hook Legends & More

Presenting some background history may help to set the mood and reasoning for some of the folklore originating from this location. Sandy Hook is a large sand spit or barrier spit, the extension of a barrier peninsula along the coast of New Jersey, separated from the mainland by the estuary of the Shrewsbury River. On its western side, the peninsula encloses Sandy Hook Bay, a triangular arm of Raritan Bay. The Dutch called the area "Sant Hoek" with the English "Hook" deriving from the Dutch "Hoek," meaning "spit of land." The peninsula was discovered by Henry Hudson and, historically, Sandy Hook has been a convenient anchorage for ships before proceeding into Upper New York Harbor.

Sandy Hook is part of Middletown Township, New Jersey, although not contiguous with the rest of the township. Because the peninsula is a federal reservation, this technicality is essentially moot. The community of Atlantic Highlands overlooks the southern part of the hook.

View of Sandy Hook.

View of Memorial at Sandy Hook.

Sandy Hook is owned by the federal government. Most of it is managed by the National Park Service as the Sandy Hook Unit of Gateway National Recreation Area. The eastern shoreline consists of public beaches: North Beach, Gunnison Beach, and South Beach. The southern part of the spit consists of public beaches and fishing areas. The peninsula's ocean-facing beaches are considered among the finest in New Jersey and are a popular destination for recreation in the summer when seasonal ferries bring beachgoers. Gunnison Beach is one of the largest clothing-optional beaches on the East Coast.

Bunkers at Sandy Hook.

The defunct U.S. Army post Fort Hancock at the north end of the peninsula is open to the public. The Sandy Hook Proving Ground was used for many years, beginning after the Civil War until 1919, when the facility was moved to Aberdeen, Maryland, and was later the site of a Nike Missile defense installation. The Sandy Hook Nike station is one of very few stations that are still intact. Almost all of the fort's gun batteries are off limits to the public due to their hazardous condition. The exception to this is Battery Gunnison, which is being restored by volunteers and has two M-1900 six-inch (152 mm) cannons installed; the weapons were placed there in 1976. Guided tours give visitors a look at an actual Nike missile, the missile firing platforms, and a radar station, complete with 1960s-era computers.

Barrack house.

Located on the peninsula are concrete bunkers, which the military built to protect the Jersey Shore from our country's enemies and used for over seventy years, from 1890 to the 1960s. The peninsula is also home to barracks and officer quarters that housed personnel, but which are no longer used for that purpose. In 1958, approximately a dozen individuals were killed as the result of a munitions explosion from a nearby base in Middletown. There is a memorial monument commemorating this sad event at Sandy Hook's Fort Hancock. It is said by many locals and visitors that if you go to the monument at midnight on the anniversary of the explosion, you can hear the sounds of the exploding munitions and the desperate cries for help of those who perished.

General Joseph Hayden Potter was a career soldier and served in the Mexican War as well as the Civil War. Even though he died at the turn-of-the-century in 1892 in Columbus, Ohio, in Sandy Hook's Fort Hancock, the main Battery Potter was named for him; does his spirit still haunt Fort Hancock, especially Battery Potter? Some locals and Park Rangers seem to think so. Many a sailor that perished on the stormy Atlantic waters off Sandy Hook were buried on this peninsula, although there were never any headstones to properly mark their graves, as these men were so far from their homes. Many visitors get the feeling of many eyes watching.

The local people of the Sandy Hook area call one of the munitions bunkers Voodoo Bunker because of cults or kids that once painted brightly vivid images that looked like Voodoo faces. It's too bad that a man accused of murdering a woman on Sandy Hook dumped the woman's body in one of the many gun batteries at Fort Hancock. When the police brought the murderer back to Fort Hancock to show them where he dumped the body, he couldn't remember which battery and to this day the woman's remains have never been recovered. Even employees at Fort Hancock claim to hear things that go bump in the night.

Sandy Hook is home to the oldest standing lighthouse in the United States. It was in operation in June 1764. Standing at ninety feet tall, it was the first lighthouse in the country to use incandescent bulbs, using electricity at the turn-of-the-nineteenth century. The location of the lighthouse and the concrete bunker, called the "Lighthouse Fort," unfortunately, was an easy target for the British during the Revolutionary War; the British eventually took control of it. Some folklore surrounding the lighthouse because of its underground passageways and secret cellar underneath the Lighthouse structures is tradition when talking about Sandy Hook.

The lightkeeper's house was excavated in the 1860s and supposedly revealed a skeleton sitting in front of a fireplace. Another version is that this skeleton was sitting at a table when discovered. In the 1960s, the Army Corps of Engineers discovered the skeletons of a woman and several men buried at the base of the Lighthouse.

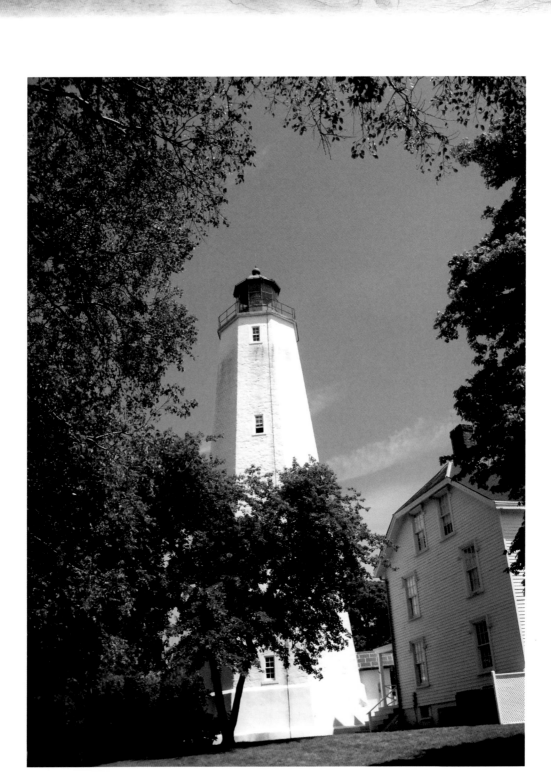

Sandy Hook Lighthouse.

Not only is the Sandy Hook Lighthouse located within the fort's grounds, but so is the Marine Academy of Science and Technology (MAST), a magnet high school, part of the Monmouth County Vocational School District. At the entrance to Fort Hancock is Guardian Park, a plaza dominated by two Nike missiles. Some of the buildings of Fort Hancock are off-limits because their structural integrity is dubious. A controversial proposal was recently accepted to allow adaptive reuse of some of the buildings in Fort Hancock for private companies; however, the developer was removed for inability to obtain financing. North of Fort Hancock is an active outpost of the United States. This area is administered by the Department of Homeland Security and is off-limits to the general public.

Capt. Huddy Reporting for Duty, Sir!

Another legend of Sandy Hook highlights Captain Joshua Huddy, a prominent resident of Colts Neck, New Jersey, and a commander of a New Jersey Patriot Militia Unit during the Revolutionary War. Huddy was assigned to protect Sandy Hook from the British, moving to and from New York City to monitor their movement. The Captain was falsely accused and hanged at the foot of the Navesink Hills on April 1782 for killing British Loyalist Philip White during a British-led attack on Sandy Hook. Even though his body was brought to Freehold, New Jersey, and is buried in Old Tennent Church's cemetery, it is rumored Huddy wanders the shores of Sandy Hook. Is he looking to exact his revenge on the British or simply continuing to protect what he was assigned to? Many people have claimed to see his spectral image frequently wandering the beach.

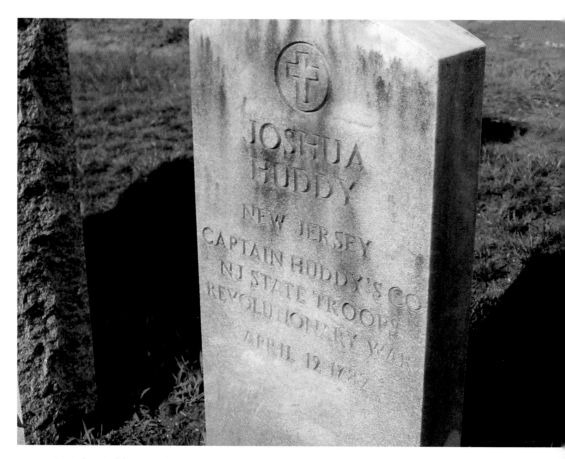

Captain Huddy gravesite.

New Jersey beaches are rich with the legends of pirates, including Captain Kidd. It is rumored Kidd buried his treasure in several locations up and down the Jersey Coast, frequently using unusual trees and other objects to navigate his way back to his ill-gotten treasures. The pines of Sandy Hook are just one of these places. Sandy Hook was the last place Kidd anchored in New Jersey before setting sail to New York on the way to Boston. To this day, Kidd and his skeleton crew have been seen dropping the anchor of their ghostly ship and roaming the shore, often dancing in the moonlit night before sailing off once again. One last hurrah, we hope your dance card isn't full.

The Legend of Mad Mary

The Navesink Light Station overlooks Sandy Hook. Built in 1764 by Charles Smith of Stonington, Connecticut, its towers' appearance was said to fulfill Smith's fantasy because he was an avid chess player. With that said, the "Twin Lights" of Navesink are unique in the way that one tower is round and one is square. Upon first look they remind you of giant pieces on a chessboard: the King and Queen. High upon the hills these Gothic-like towers loom two hundred feet above sea level; over time the Twin Lights have had over twelve lightkeepers and more than seventy assistants.

One legend that is known is of "Mad" Mary Coyle. Mary's husband Thomas was one of the assistant lightkeepers; he died from pneumonia while serving the lighthouse. Mary decided she would return to her roots in Ireland since there was nothing left for her here in New Jersey, but during her last night spent in the Twin Lights, out of growing heartbreak and grief, she climbed up to the lamp room in the North Tower and threw herself off the tower — two hundred feet on the rocks below — to her certain death. Many visitors have claimed to see Mary in the stairwell just around dusk, but when asked, employees say they don't know about the legend. Could it be that they don't want anyone to know for fear of frightening visitors away?

Haunting view of Sandy Hook's Twin Lights.

Chapter 15

Robin Hood of the Pine Barrens

There is no 'Band of Merry Men' connected to this piece of folklore; however, few figures in South Jersey's history have more tales and myths attached to them than the Tory outlaw, Joe Mulliner, often referred to as the "Robin Hood of the Pine Barrens." His was a most unusual career, related over and over through the centuries, with more details added with each retelling, but Joe Mulliner was real and his exploits during the time of the Revolutionary War were legendary. How much of his life's tale is true and how much is myth is for the reader to decide.

In one piece of folklore, purported to have taken place in the forgotten and lost town of Washington, New Jersey, buried deep in the Wharton State Forest, another Mulliner legend was born. On the old stage road from Quaker Bridge to Tuckerton lies the ruin of an old stable that for many years was misidentified as the ruins of the renowned Washington Tavern. The actual site of the tavern is less than a half-mile east on the opposite side of the road, where all that remains is a depression in the ground that marks the location of the cellar. One day Mulliner made his way towards the back door of the tavern in search of some refreshment. On the way he passed a young woman crying in the backyard. When he inquired as to the cause of her troubles, his appearance frightened her and she ran into the inn. Mulliner followed and soon discovered the cause of her unhappiness — a forced betrothal. He waited for the start of the ceremony before appearing on the stairway with his guns brandished to stop the marriage. He gave the groom one of two choices: leave or die. The groom chose the former and was never seen again. Risking arrest, Mulliner stayed until nightfall, drinking and dancing too much, but not leaving until every woman present had a turn on the dance floor with him.

Like many of the towns and villages that once existed in the vast expanse of the New Jersey Pine Barrens, Joe Mulliner's grave has now disappeared. There is little physical evidence remaining of the legendary leader of the Refugee gang. Even his ghost is no longer seen about the countryside. However, among the heavy growth of trees along the old stage roads in Wharton State Forest, you can feel the apprehension travelers must have felt when Mulliner was on the loose. Unable to see clearly very far in any direction, you can understand how easily a stage could be surprised. The remoteness of the area makes you realize how alone you would be if stopped by the outlaw. You can still sense the spirit of Joe Mulliner. He would still feel right at home here.

The *New Jersey Gazette* of August 8, 1781, reported:

> "At a special court lately held in Burlington, a certain Joseph Mulliner, of Egg-Harbor, was convicted of high treason, and is sentenced to be hanged this very day. This fellow had become the terror of that part of country. He had made a practice of burning houses, robbing and plundering all who fell in his way, so that when he came to trial it appeared the whole country, both Whigs and Tories, were his enemy."

Mulliner was taken from his jail cell and transported, his own coffin in the wagon with him, to nearby Gallows Hill. There the career of New Jersey's most famous Refugee came to a final end. His body was sent home to his wife and buried on the family farm he had been forced to flee from just three short years earlier. His grave was marked with a simple small stone reading "JM." However, he did not rest easily. Travelers along the old stage roads would report hearing booming laughter in the woods or seeing a large man standing in the roadway with guns drawn. Others would report a lone ghostly figure walking along the banks of the Mullica River near The Forks. In 1850, some drunken workers from nearby Batso dug up his bones, but Jesse Richards, the Ironmaster of the village, had them returned for proper reburial. The grave then remained unchanged and rarely visited until the 1930s, when a local sportsmen's club installed a more proper headstone. It read: "The Grave of Joe Mulliner — Hung 1781."

Is Joe still hanging around…why not find out for yourself?

Chapter 16

"Der Fuhrer" Dying in New Jersey

WWII Revived

Could it be true that "Der Fuhrer" Adolf Hitler escaped to New Jersey and lived right under our noses? I guess anything may have been possible given the confusion at the end of the Second World War.

Let's examine the segments of the story beginning with a patient of an area nursing home that was in close proximity to Lakewood, New Jersey. The patient, in his early eighties at the time, was transported to a Toms River hospital emergency room and admitted for a severe hip problem. Delirious at the time, a nurse's aide passing by two nurses standing outside his room overheard them talking. The information heard by the nurse's aide was startling: One nurse was telling the other that when she attended to the man he was mumbling, in his delirious state, the words in fluent German "Ich bein Hitler," translated meaning "I am Hitler." He mumbled these words several times before succumbing to his illness.

This incident allegedly took place in late 1979 and the dying gentleman was said to have been approximately ninety years in age. Adolph Hitler was born in 1889 and one could easily conclude that both he and the gentleman would have been of the same age.

During his military service in the First World War, Hitler had received a severe upper thigh wound in the same leg as the gentleman had; this type of wound in later years could conceivably cause a serious hip problem. The gentleman never regained consciousness and still, today this story is mentioned in hushed tones. When you give this some thought, is it possible? We may never really know, but if fact and not fiction, he could not have lived his remaining years in a better environment.

As an addendum to this interesting piece of New Jersey folklore, being a serious researcher myself, my interest has always been aroused when Adolf Hitler and the closing days of the Second World War are the subject of any discussion. The question lingered in my mind; did Adolf Hitler really die in the bunker as history has portrayed this situation? I am certain that many of the statements surrounding his death were in fact true in the minds of those who believed them to be or had been perceived to be. Circumstances at that time seem to back up the statements.

Adolf Hitler's death has never, beyond all doubt, been sustained other than by the Russians and certain "loyal" members of Der Fuhrer's staff, so were they really believable? At the time I would have to say yes, as this is what the world wanted to believe.

Research has indicated that Erich Kempka, Hitler's loyal driver, had never observed the faces of the two bodies, rolled in blankets, that were brought to him in the tiny courtyard of the Reichchancellory before setting them on fire, allegedly at Hitler's orders. During the last days of the war, Hitler made a decision to remain in the bunker until the end, again so we have been told. I have discovered two incidents that may make one view this "last ditch death" situation from a different perspective. Adolf Hitler's trusted personal pilot SS General Hans Bauer, who would have been the logical choice to fly Der Fuhrer out of Germany as originally planned, was released by Hitler along with several others, to make their way on foot away from the Russian troops as they were entering Berlin. This decision would lead one to believe he had remained. Hans Bauer was captured on the streets of Berlin with Hitler's secretary Gertrud "Traudl" Junge and possibly two others.

Another unusual situation began on April 25, 1945, involving Germany's foremost pilot Colonel Hans Ulrich Rudel, who was ordered to fly into Berlin. The following is an excerpt from his book *Stuka Pilot*.

"On 25 April another (second) wireless signal from the Fhurer's headquarters (in the bunker) reaches me, completely jumbled. Practically nothing is intelligible, but I assume I am again being summoned to Berlin. I ring up the air command and report that I have been presumably ordered to Berlin and requested permission to fly there. The commodore refuses, according to the army bulletin fighting is going on around the Templehof Aerodrome (airfield) and he does not know if there is any airfield free of the enemy. He says, if you come down in the Russian lines they will chop my head off for having allowed you to start (fly there). He says he will try to contact Wing Commander Nicolaus von Below immediately by wireless to ask for the correct text of the message and where I can land, if at all.

For some days I hear nothing, then at eleven in the evening on the 27th April he rings me up to inform me that he has at last made contact with Berlin and that I am to fly there tonight in a Heinkel 111 and land on the wide east-to-west arterial road through Berlin at the point where the Brandenburg Gate and the Victory monuments stand. Niermann will accompany me."

The rest is fairly simple: he landed at Wittstock to refuel, continued to Berlin, and landed as ordered. Shortly after he landed, another officer informing him that he was to wait here pending further orders from Hitler approached him. As time passed, moments seemed like hours and finally the same officer returned, telling him that Hitler had decided to remain in the bunker until the end and that he was to now fly back to his base, take his Stuka wing, and lead them to the nearest American airfield and surrender himself and them to the Americans.

Now give this some thought: Who better than the most highly decorated and respected (by both his American and British counterparts) Stuka pilot of the German Luftwaffe to carry this scenario out? He had told them the truth after surrendering himself and other members of his wing so as not to be taken by the Russians, who, by the way, had a high price on his head for several years of the war for his capture.

What very few, if any, other than Hitler himself, knew is that he had a backup pilot to Hans Bauer. Was Der Fuhrer flown out of Germany? If so, where did he go? If this narrative just presented is proven to be true, this could be considered as the ultimate illusion of the twentieth century and should command an Oscar for the best performance by a crumbling dictatorship.

Chapter 17

Telegraph Tower
Still Speaking — Loud and Clear!

Mystic Island's Little Secret

The area that is currently Mystic Island was once called Hickory Island and was serviced by the Tuckerton Railroad and one two-laned street named Shore Road, which was later renamed Radio Road after the Tuckerton Wireless Tower.

The Tuckerton Wireless Tower was built in 1912 by the German Hochfrequenzmaschinen Aktiengesellschaft fur Drahtlose Telegraphie Company. The High Frequency Machine Corporation for Wireless Telegraphy was often referred to as HOMAG, when the present-day Mystic Island was called Hickory Island. The tower was used to communicate with an identical radio telegraph station in Eilvese, Germany, starting on June 19, 1914, less than two weeks before the assassination of Archduke Ferdinand. The station continued to communicate with Eilvese until America entered World War One on April 6, 1917. It has been rumored that it was used to send the message ordering the attack by a German U-boat on the *RMS Lusitania*.

After President Wilson's Declaration of Neutrality, the President ordered the US Navy to take over the station on September 9, 1914, to assure the neutrality of messages sent to and from the station; however, the station was still operated by German nationals employed by HOMAG and who continued communications only with the Eilvese radio station. When America entered the war, all U.S. radio stations were seized and shut down by Executive Order and the Tuckerton Radio Station was assigned to the US Navy, which used it primarily to back-up the communications of the US Navy's main transatlantic radio station in New Brunswick, New Jersey. The German personnel remaining at Tuckerton became war prisoners and were replaced by Navy personnel.

Along Radio Road, just a short distance from the beaches of Gravelling Point in Little Egg Harbor, stands this piece of New Jersey history, an oddity amidst the aging developments of Mystic Island. Some errant residents spray-painted the remains of the tower, marking its foundation as a true relic of yesterday. Three concrete blocks, twenty feet below the earth and twenty-four feet aboveground, stand as remnants of one of the tallest telegraphic towers in history. These three huge anchor blocks still exist today, in a backyard on North Ensign Drive and in the middle of South Ensign Drive and Storysail Drive. Many smaller anchor blocks providing foundations for smaller towers that supported the umbrella antenna are still visible in the lagoons. Remains of the tower can be viewed in scraps at the Giffordtown Museum. Although observers may find the artifacts simple and meaningless relics, this unusual tower was reported to have played a part in the defeat of the British passenger liner *Lusitania*, an event that helped to spur the United States into War World I.

As war broke out in Europe in 1914, the tower was believed to have been used for war purposes by Germany, which resulted in a public outcry from both England and France. Although President Wilson forbade the use of the tower for contacting ships at sea, the Tuckerton tower had communicated sailing information to the German cruisers *Dresden* and *Karlsruhe*. Joseph Daniels, Secretary of the Navy, enforced an operational takeover of the tower with nine enlisted men assigned to handle transmissions, although German workers remained for maintenance purposes. During 1915, newspapers printed a warning from the Imperial German Government stating: "Travelers intending to embark on the Atlantic voyage are reminded that a state of war exists between Germany and Great Britain; that the zone of war includes the waters adjacent to the British Isles. Vessels flying the flag of Great Britain, or her allies, are liable to destruction in those waters."

Soon after, the commander of the Imperial German submarine U-20 received a message, Get Lucy, allegedly sent from the Tuckerton wireless tower; 1,198 lives were lost as the *Lusitania* was torpedoed as it arrived on the British coast. By 1917, all German employees of the Tuckerton tower were ordered to leave and the U.S. declared war on Germany on April 6, 1917. Secret Service men arrived in Tuckerton, placing the remaining German staff under arrest. Solely the U.S. government for the rest of the war then used the tower.

To this day, although no longer in existence, residents and visitors to the site come away with claims of hearing conversation in a foreign language, some recognizing it as being German. Are these alleged voices simply residue from a bygone period in time or just a part of one's imagination? Either way, the story has stood the test of time, as many visitors to the New Jersey Shore seek out this site with the hope of hearing a word or two from history.

Chapter 18

Cape May or 'May Not'

Legend of the Cape May Diamond

At Cape May Point was the tribal headquarters of the Kechemeche Indians, a component of the Lenni-Lenape Council. These Indians were blood affiliates of the Algonquin Nation, a peace loving tribe of aborigines.

The Kechemeche were the first to find the beautiful translucent stones known as "Cape May Diamonds." The gems were found in limited areas on the beach along Delaware Bay. The Indians, who attracted mystical powers and a sacred trust to their possession, held these gems in high esteem. The Kechemeche believed these curious stones possessed supernatural powers, influencing the success, well-being, and good fortune of the possessor.

The bonds of friendship and lasting good will were often sealed with the gift or exchange of these beautiful sacred gems. This was especially true of those gems that were larger and free of any flaws. King Nummy, last chief of the Lenni-Lenape, presented one of the largest "Cape May Diamonds" to an early settler, Christopher Leaming. King Nummy received the gem from the Kechemeche as a tribute to him and as proof of their faithfulness and loyalty.

Mr. Leaming had the stone sent back to the old country. In Amsterdam, Holland, a lapidary expertly cut and polished it into a most beautiful gem. These beautiful gems we know as "Cape May Diamonds" are pure quartz crystals thrown by tides to appear as pebbles on the beach. Quartz is the most common of minerals, coming in a variety of colors.

The source of the "Cape May Diamonds" is the upper reaches of the Delaware River, some two hundred miles upstream, where for thousands of years the swift waters have eroded away pockets and veins of quartz crystal. They then begin the long journey to the ocean, taking thousands of years to complete. Upon reaching the mouth of the Delaware Bay, some seventeen miles across, they are propelled swiftly. This is because the belly of the Bay is twenty-six miles across, causing a strong flow on both incoming and outgoing tides. This strong flow comes against the sides of the concrete ship *Atlantis*, which swirls the Quartz pebbles ashore, along with other material, including fossil sharks' teeth and Indian arrowheads. The larger stones come ashore mostly in the winter months when the surf is considerably stronger, particularly during storms.

Cape May Lighthouse turned 150 years old on October 31, 2009.

The "Cape May Diamond" comes in a variety of sizes; finds as large as eggs have been reported. On one occasion, a gem weighing over one pound was found. When polished or cut and faceted, these gems have the appearance of a genuine diamond. When finished, "Cape May Diamonds" can be mounted in gold, silver, or platinum, creating beautiful jewelry items. Before the advent of modern gem-scanning equipment, a "Cape May Diamond" fooled many a pawnbroker. The "Cape May Diamonds" are found in abundance along the beach in historic Cape May Point. From early spring until late fall, visitors come by the thousands to collect "Cape May Diamonds," fossils, and Indian artifacts in the shadow of the concrete ship *Atlantis*.

Built during the First World War, the *Atlantis* was an experimental ship. Due to its extreme weight, the result of being constructed of concrete, the ship proved not to be practical. Eventually, the ship was permanently docked at Cape May Point and during a severe storm broke from its mooring and began to sink just offshore. Only a small part of the ship still remains visible above the surface and those who linger on Sunset Beach toward evening claim to hear the sounds of moaning and groaning at times when the air is still. Is this simply the mind playing tricks or is there more to this myth? Only time will tell — after the *Atlantis* eventually completes its journey to its final resting place at the ocean bottom.

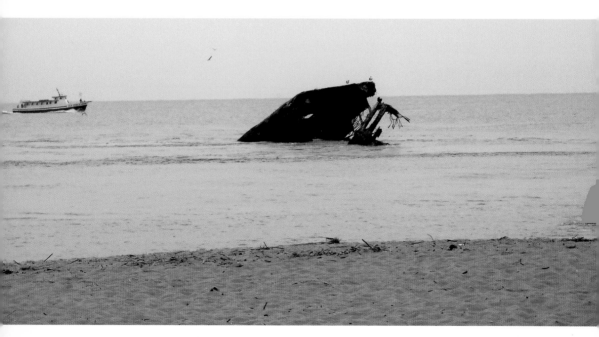

Cape May Concrete Ship.

A word of warning: As the tale goes, should you venture on Sunset Beach or "Diamond Beach" at sunset you may encounter King Nummy himself or what appears to be his shadow standing facing the setting sun—or is it simply a tale?

Cape May Sunset Beach view.

Cape May Submarine Watchtower

This watchtower was used as a lookout to spot German submarines during World War II. According to Cape May County Park employees, a submarine was spotted and sank in Delaware Bay. Supposedly it is still there to this day they say. Legend has it that at certain times ghostly images can be seen seemingly still searching for German submarines.

Haunted watchtower still standing tall.

The Bermuda Triangle & the Cape May Connection

Within the past century an interesting story has resonated from the Cape May area centered around the so-called 'Bermuda Triangle', a rather vaguely defined area of the North Atlantic Ocean that has, over time, gained a sinister reputation as being unusually dangerous and mysterious. This reputation is due to the fact that, according to some, an abnormally large number of ships and aircraft have disappeared in what are strange, inexplicable, and even unnatural circumstances. As a result of such claims the area has attracted a number of rather melodramatic designations such as the Deadly Triangle, the Hoodoo Sea, the Devil's Triangle, the Twilight Zone, the Triangle of Death, Limbo of the Lost, and the Graveyard of the Atlantic. However, the term by which it is best known, the Bermuda Triangle, came from the title of a fictional story, "*The Deadly Bermuda Triangle,*" written by Gaddis in 1974.

The actual shape and area of the triangle are, however, somewhat elastic and, over time, various authors have 'stretched' the borders of the triangle to enable them to include disappearances from locations far beyond the areas originally defined. The principal outlines proposed for the Bermuda Triangle are now considered a triangle bounded roughly by Florida, Bermuda, and Puerto Rico, an amorphous formation commencing at Cape May and extending out to the edge of the continental shelf, following the East Coast around the Florida peninsula into the Gulf of Mexico and includes the islands of Cuba, Jamaica, and Dominica.

Should this scenario have even the slightest ounce of reality, it would account for some of the sightings of strange events along the southernmost stretches of the New Jersey shoreline, the folklore spoken from the lips of New Jerseyans living in shore areas, and what the many summer visitors bring home with them as part of their souvenirs.

Cape May's Higbee Beach

This stretch of beach on the bay side of Cape May is one of the most beautiful beaches there and well worth the extra effort it takes to see it. The dunes, trees, and brush here have been preserved to provide a habitat for birds. It is easy to imagine Captain Kidd or Blackbeard burying treasure there in the dead of the night. The ghosts at Higbee are not pirates, though. Some say the ghost is Mr. Higbee; other legends claim the ghost is Higbee's slave, who kept a vigil at his grave after his master's death. It is a place that holds an eerie, desolate feeling, especially in autumn.

Dead Giant

This dead giant off Cape May beach is an abandoned World War Two concrete bunker, now several yards offshore due to beach erosion of past years. Located just east of the Cape May Point Lighthouse in what is now Cape May Point State Park, the bunker was built by the United States Army Corps of Engineers during the early months of the Second World War. It contained heavy artillery and was manned by a rotating detail of naval gunnery crews who spent hours scanning the horizon for enemy surface ships and submarines. In fact, a German U-Boat commander surrendered his vessel just off the coast of Cape May at the end of World War Two.

This bunker was part of a coastal defense system during World War II. In front of this bunker were 6" turrets and 155MM guns. The bunker was originally nine hundred feet inland. Coastal erosion has taken its toll on the beach. As legend would have it, some on-lookers say that just after sunset if you listen carefully you may hear voices coming from the bunker and shadows of what appear to be men walking about.

Chapter 19

The Elusive "Jersey Devil"

Let's start with the term "Pineys." Allegedly poor, backwoods folk living in Southern portions of New Jersey coupled with inferior genetics. This particular piece of folklore begins with the Leeds family, one of the earlier settlers to the area. The Leeds family resided in Atlantic County, particularly May's Landing, over 275 years ago. Some say as early as the eighteenth century, in the year 1735. It was said that Jane Leeds perhaps dabbled in witchcraft to escape the reality of being not well-off; her husband was somewhat of a heavy drinker and she had twelve children to contend with. This all sounds fairly normal probably for that time period, but the story becomes a little stranger.

Jersey Devil. *Artwork by Brian Kovacs.*

Jane Leeds was pregnant with her thirteenth child, which put an even larger strain on the family; after all, it was another mouth to feed, another child to rear, and no husband to help her. Some say she was never married and was nothing more than a whore. As for the thirteenth child, a midwife delivered a boy on a rainy night in January. Either when Jane discovered she was pregnant or during the delivery, she shouted the words: "Let this one be the devil!" or "Let the devil take this one!" The baby transformed into this devil-like creature, killed the midwife, and flew up the chimney. Other accounts are that the child was left to die in the basement, but eventually escaped. Not your typical childbirth. Some say she made a pact with Satan himself in exchange for eternal youth, some say she was cursed by having a thirteenth child.

This cryptic has been repeated by hundreds of people, including reputable sources, describing this creature as having the head of a horse, large bat-like wings, claws, and hooves. It wasn't until around 1909 that you started hearing reports of people being terrorized by this devil. Livestock was being suspiciously killed, even milk souring. Imagine that. Is it possible a child transformed and roams the Pine Barrens? The Philadelphia Zoo in Pennsylvania even offered a reward for the capture of this creature to be housed at the Zoo, but no one came forth with this beast. In the 1950s, the fears of Jersey Shore residents were heightened once again when a corpse bearing a striking resemblance to what hundreds of witnesses have reported over the last two hundred or so years surfaced. Could such a creature live for more than 275 years? Is it possible this creature has reproduced over the centuries?

Being paranormal investigators and lifelong residents of New Jersey, our interest cannot help but be peaked about something that has become so commercialized and naturally we want to want to investigate this. If this creature still exists, it would make for one heck of an investigation. A colleague and fellow investigator in Asbury Park owns a bookstore that only sells books on the paranormal and related subjects. She has also started a museum, largely of interesting facts and material on the Jersey Devil, so that is where we decided to start digging.

View of Leeds property site where the home that was the birthplace of the Jersey Devil once stood.

Investigation

It would be difficult, but not impossible, to spend a great deal of man hours covering the many Jersey Shore towns spanning several counties searching for the Jersey Devil. However, there are people that absolutely dedicate their lives to doing just this, but NJGO decided that we would pick our battles and concentrate on investigating only a small portion of Devil Country – for now. We thought we would set out to see where this all began. Sometimes you have to go back in order to go forward, so given the history of the Jersey Devil and how widely known this "lore" is it is totally impossible for any one of our psychics to go into something like this cold. We would have to rely mostly on equipment. Anything we did receive from the psychic would be absolutely helpful and could support any shred of evidence we may get.

Perhaps their guidance in a specific area could be useful; after all, they have the ability to know when something that we cannot see ourselves is present. It is all certainly worth trying. Our road trip began, where else, but at the Atlantic City casinos. A little unwinding couldn't hurt before beginning. When in Rome… is the old saying. Atlantic City was a base for us to go back to in between the places we planned on investigating.

We located the Leeds property, but to our dismay nothing visible remained. We spoke to some locals who know some Leeds' family descendants and we had the correct location. We had even spoken to a shop owner on the boardwalk in Atlantic City. He was brought up with the story surrounding the Jersey Devil and lived in the area we had explored, so we were partly satisfied that we had come that far. That's where it all began — off the beaten path, in a small town, deep in the woods — and it was a full moon coming that evening. It couldn't make for a better trip that day. How many people can say they came that close? If I wasn't convinced that this "lore" was true, I was now. I guess you will have to explore for yourself… Just don't get lost in the Pine Barrens.

Authors' Note: According to Lenape legend, the dense wilderness, which covers over a million acres in southern New Jersey that we now know as the Pinelands, was home of the Mahtantu, a destructive, evil being that they associated with the Devil. This belief far predates the legend of Mother Leeds' giving birth to her thirteenth child, who transformed into the *Jersey Devil*, the horned and winged beast of the Pinelands.

Chapter 20

Pirates

"Dem Bones"

Treasure Lake at Cliffwood Beach and Money Island in Toms River are named for local legends of pirate visitation and the shore has stories of Captain Kidd's landfalls that are virtually identical to tales from North Carolina to Canada. Kidd's 1699 attempt to finesse his way back into New York and obtain a royal pardon involved leaving a small stash on Gardiner's Island, which was apparently recovered by Colonial authorities. His subsequent trial and execution in England inspired stories that say undiscovered loot remains all over the East Coast.

The early nineteenth century press and penny novelists pitched endless stories about "Barnegat pirates" and "moon-cussers," who allegedly used false night signals to lure ships onto shoals so they would be wrecked and open to looting.

Dem Bones are the skeletal crew of Captain Kidd. According to folklore, they sail up in a ship made of shadows. As Kidd's ship, *Adventure Galley*, moves silently up the coast at the dark of the moon and anchors near the shores of Sandy Hook, two or three boats are lowered from her side — and filled with the eager forms of glowing skeletons wearing cocked hats and tattered buccaneers garb. Around their waists are belts full of pistols and long cutlasses. The biggest of the Dem Bones, the one that is probably the first mate, has a skeletal parrot perched on his shoulder.

Dem Bones carries heavy trunks full of treasure onto the shore, scatters it all around where the pine grove once stood, and then hauls out kegs and kegs of whiskey. One of the skeletons takes out a fiddle, a phantom fire is lit on the sand, and Dem Bones start such a rowdy singing and dancing that the noise would wake the dead — if they weren't already awake. When they are exhausted from the dancing, the glowing skeletons collapse on the sand and start telling stories about the ships they have captured and the treasure they have amassed. Some Dem Bones open the big trunks and take out jewels and ropes of pearls and adorn themselves. Others toss gold coins back and forth as if they were a child's ball. At the darkest part of the night, just before dawn, the Dem Bones pack up the trunks and row back to the ship of shadows. One by one, the glowing skeletons disappear into the hold and the ship draws anchor and sails away.

A place believed to contain Captain Kidd's treasure is in the area of Del Haven — recently discovered maps and documents point to a site directly under a commercial professional complex of buildings. The treasure, if it were there at all, would be located beneath the concrete foundations of the structures.

A more romantic story concerning the famed pirate captain is that he became enamored with an Ocean County lass known only as Amanda. She persuaded Captain Kidd to abandon his uncertain, although colorful, career and settle in the wilds of South Jersey. In preparation for this move, he decided to divide much of the available loot with the crew and bury the rest on Brigantine. His ship was anchored in the mouth of the Mullica River when he was betrayed by an unsatisfied crewmember and had to make a run for it out to sea. Captain Kidd made well his escape, but was captured in the vicinity of Boston in late 1699 and sent to England for trial. Charged with piracy and murder, Captain Kidd was found guilty and hanged in London on May 24, 1701, protesting his innocence to the last. If these additional buried treasures actually existed, Amanda and her captain kept their final resting place an external secret. The cache has never been found.

Stede Bonnet's treasure is rumored to be buried at a point somewhere along the Delaware Bay, perhaps, as some sources indicate, in the vicinity north of the Cape May-Lewes Ferry Terminal. Though sources indicate it was buried near the original settlement of Town Bank, it could very well lie beneath the waves now as the village has been flooded by natural erosion.

During the sixteenth and seventeenth centuries, some locals told stories of the ghost of Kidd walking along the beach with the Jersey Devil. In these reports, Kidd is often headless.

Kidd started out actually fairly wealthy. He was a merchant and settled in what is now Manhattan. He basically owned Manhattan, but he was looking for more. Not that he was greedy, but he knew he wanted to do something different. He returned to England and became a Privateer, commissioned by the King of England to hunt pirates and enemies to the British Throne. To make a long story short, failing to meet deadlines in Madagascar and capturing no pirates, he returned to the Red Sea and remained there for months, just sailing. It was during that time that the line between being a Privateer and a pirate became fuzzy. The only difference was a piece of paper making being a Privateer legal. Eventually Kidd became desperate and took whatever ships he could, legal or not, agreement papers or not. Or did he? When he was captured and eventually tried in England, the papers he did hold disappeared. He was hanged. Some say the trial was purposely stacked against him. The papers in question were discovered hundreds of years later. Some say he was used as a pawn by England to strengthen their position against their war with France, so was Kidd a pirate after all?

Pirate Treasure Map

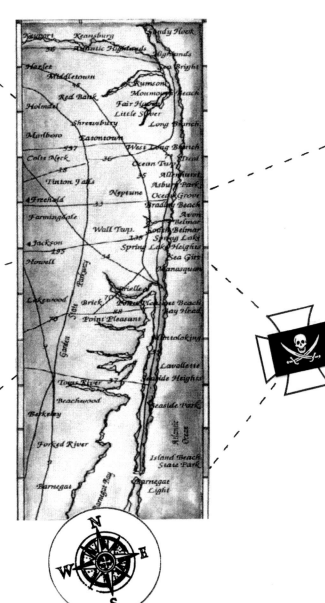

The Never-ending Search for Treasure

Before Captain Kidd's death by hanging, he was insistent on mentioning another fabulous treasure hidden elsewhere. The "elsewhere" is rumored to be on Money Island, which is now Cliffwood Beach, New Jersey. Could this be true? Many a seventeenth century Spanish gold coin has been sighted on these beaches according to the local people.

One person, William S. Horner, a past Monmouth County Historian, seemed to think differently.

Pirates preferred to bury their booty rather than risk arrest or, worse, death. Two pirates may have stayed on in Monmouth County; some were tried, some returned to England, and some just disappeared into thin air. Moses Butterworth supposedly disappeared and was last seen heading towards the Raritan Bay. In other stories long passed down, many locals in the area spoke of an old man who lived in the Atlantic Highlands. Could this have been Moses Butterworth?

William Leeds turned in his pirate hat and became a very wealthy, very generous, and respected citizen in Middletown, New Jersey. Leeds claimed he knew where Captain Kidd's treasure was buried. Local people felt that this booty accounted for Leeds' wealth. Some people claim he had wisely invested this ill-gotten fortune when upon his death he left his entire estate of land to the Christ Church. Local folklore tells of parishioners actually seeing the treasure chest. Leeds is buried at the Christ Church cemetery in Shrewsbury.

Did these left-behind pirates from bygone eras know the inside scoop on real treasure or is that wishful thinking on the part of New Jerseyans? No one ever stops looking on the Jersey Shores.

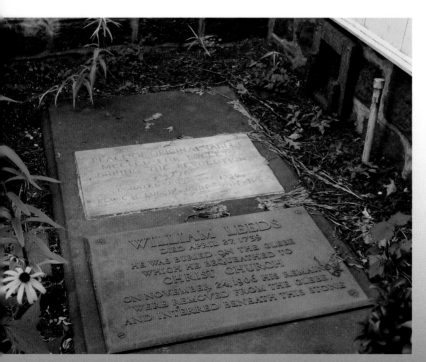

William Leeds gravesite (not related to the Jersey Devil Leeds).

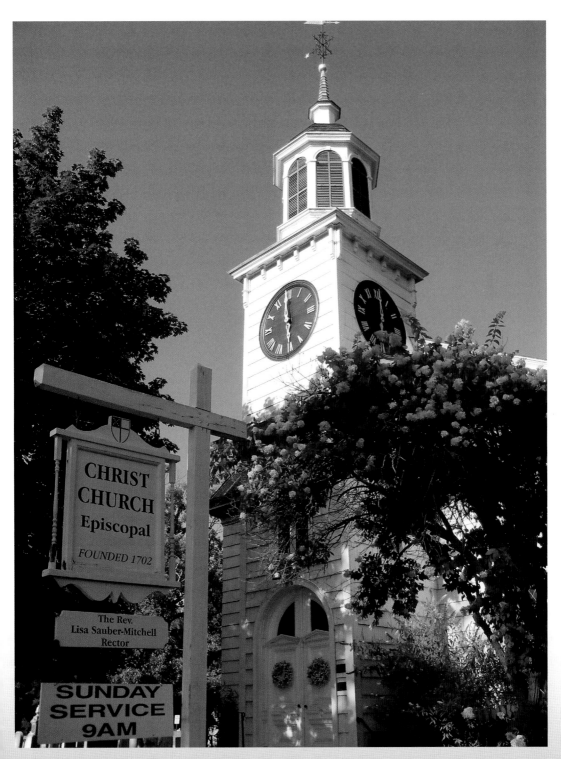

Christ Church, site of William Leeds gravesite.

Middletown Myth

Edward Teach, also known as Blackbeard, was not the most successful pirate or the most vicious or violent. Although he was not exceptional, his tall stature and thick long black beard with twisted braids and colorful ribbons intertwined could strike fear in the bravest of his enemies and victims alike without harm. Make no mistake — his reputation was cemented by his frightening appearance. It has been said that Teach stuck lighted matches under his hat to emphasize this look.

After being ambushed off the coast of North Carolina, he met a gruesome death. He was shot many times, culminating with many cuts by sword. He was decapitated, his body thrown into the Atlantic Ocean. His head was kept and suspended from one of the ship's sails as the ship remained anchored.

In 1997, the wreckage of Blackbeard's ship, the *Queen Anne's Revenge*, was located and brought to the surface. Many a story has circulated that the ghost of Blackbeard is seen roaming the afterlife searching for his severed head. Unexplained flickering lights with no apparent source have been recounted from locals spanning the eastern coast. Have these pirates come back to unearth their loot?

It is most likely the Jersey Coast was a convenient place to come ashore to replenish basic supplies, including water, ammunition, and livestock, before setting sail back to Europe. Middletown was no exception. If you ask any local in Middletown, they will tell you Blackbeard terrorized the residents on their farms for just this purpose. However, there has never been proof to backup this story and over time it has been rated high among the area residents.

Blackbeard's Buried Burlington Treasure

As late as 1875 an enormous black walnut stump remained on the east side of Wood Street, just North of Union in Burlington, New Jersey, as a reminder of buried pirate treasure. One dark and stormy night, believed early inhabitants, Blackbeard and his pirate crew landed at the foot of Wood Street with their gold and silver plunder in search of a location to bury their treasure. Beneath that walnut tree, they buried their bloodstained gains under a broad, flat stone, and under a suicidal Spanish cutthroat who volunteered when Blackbeard cried above the storm, "Who'll guard this wealth?" A charmed bullet left no wound, but did the deed, and they buried the pirate upright, feet resting on the stone he guarded. The ship's dog must have been partial to the Spaniard, because it was shot, too, and buried there. For many years into the twentieth century, folks on Wood Street reported seeing a black dog, guarding the tree, and then vanishing.

Now, some say he returned to claim his treasure one wild stormy night, but that the lightning flashes from the storm revealed a spectacle of haggard witches dancing with linked hands around the Spaniard's grave, forever repelling the superstitious pirates.

Black Dog

Folklore is not the only 'tail' wagging; another old Pine Barren story tells of the Black Dog, a ghostly creature that roamed the beaches and forests from Absecon Island to Barnegat Bay. In most folklore (such as English and Germanic folklore), Black Dogs are considered forces of evil. In fact there is an English legend akin to this. However, the Black Dog of the Pine Barren is often considered a harmless spirit. According to folklore, pirates on Absecon Island attacked a ship and killed its crew. Among those killed were the cabin boy and his black dog.

Chapter 21

"Molly" — Water!

Molly Pitcher was a nickname given to a woman said to have fought in the American Revolutionary War. Since various Molly Pitcher tales grew in the telling, many historians regard Molly Pitcher as folklore rather than history or suggest that Molly Pitcher may be a composite image inspired by the actions of a number of real women. The name itself may have originated as a nickname given to women who carried water to men on the battlefield during the war.

At the Battle of Monmouth in June 1778, Mary Hays tended to the Revolutionary soldiers by giving them water. Just before the battle started, she found a spring to serve as her water supply. (Actually, two places on the battlefield are currently marked as the "Molly Pitcher Spring.") Mary Hays spent much of the early day carrying water to soldiers and artillerymen, often under heavy fire from British troops.

The weather was hot, over 100 degrees Fahrenheit. Sometime during the battle, William Hays collapsed next to his cannon. He was either wounded or collapsed from heat exhaustion. (It has often been reported that Hays was killed in the battle, but it is known that he survived.) As her husband was carried off the battlefield, Mary Hays took his place at the cannon. For the rest of the day, in the heat of battle, Mary continued to "swab and load" the cannon using her husband's rammer. At one point, a British musket ball or cannon ball flew between her legs and tore off the bottom of her skirt. Mary supposedly said, "Well, that could have been worse," and went back to loading the cannon.

Later in the evening, the fighting ceased due to gathering darkness. Although George Washington and his commanders expected the battle to continue the following day, the British forces retreated during the night and continued on to Sandy Hook, New Jersey. The battle was seen as a major victory for the Continental Army.

At the conclusion of the battle, General Washington asked about the woman who he had seen loading a cannon on the battlefield. In commemoration for her courage, Washington issued Mary Hays a warrant as a non-commissioned officer. Afterwards, she was known as "Sergeant Molly," a nickname that she used for the rest of her life.

Monmouth Battlefield, general view of the cannon area at the time of the battle.

There is a hotel in Red Bank, New Jersey, not far from the site of the Battle of Monmouth, called the Molly Pitcher Inn. Close by the site, in Freehold, New Jersey, there is a small stone marker that purports to indicate the location of Molly Pitcher's well. This marker is for the benefit of tourists; it is said the actual location of the well is a slight distance away from the marker.

Another probable source for the legend of "Molly Pitcher" is the true story of Margaret Corbin, which bears many similarities to the story of Mary Hays. Margaret Corbin was the wife of John Corbin of Philadelphia, also an artilleryman in the Continental army. On November 12, 1776, John Corbin was one of 2,800 American soldiers who defended Fort Washington in northern Manhattan from 9,000 attacking Hessian troops under British command. When John Corbin was killed, Margaret took his place at the cannon, continuing to fire until she was seriously wounded in the arm. In 1779, Margaret Corbin was awarded an annual pension by the state of Pennsylvania for her heroism in battle. She was the first woman in the United States to receive a military pension. Her nickname was "Captain Molly."

Chapter 22

The Less Traveled Roads

The Legend of the Buckeyes

The most infamous legends at the Jersey Shore no doubt are Captain William Kidd, the pirate from England who buried his legendary treasures up and down the New Jersey coast, and the Jersey Devil that terrorized folks primarily in the Pine Barren towns of Southern New Jersey. However, did you know that there are many more folklore stories and urban legends you may not have heard of? Here are a few that may hold your attention.

This urban legend has its origins on the Delaware River, near Washington's Crossing. Lambertville High School, overlooking the Delaware River, was built in 1854, but a major fire in 1926 destroyed most of the school and possibly killed 150 students. Although the school was rebuilt the following year, another fire raged, destroying the third floor. It is unclear how far back this legend goes. There was a championship football game between the Lambertville team and the New Hope Buckeyes (New Hope, Pennsylvania, just across the river). During this important game, one of the Buckeye players was tackled. After the dust settled and all of the players involved in the play got up, the tackled boy (Billy) lay still on the field…dead. His neck was broken and his head completely turned around. The parents of the New Hope team players felt so strongly about the tragedy that eventually football was removed from the school curriculum even to present day. Lambertville School was eventually closed in 1959 and a new, more modern one was built nearby.

School was out in the 1990s when yet another fire occurred, this time at the hands of vandals. Its ominous presence of remains stands high up on Coryell's Hill (better known as High School Hill), the highest hill in the town. The town originally purchased land (now the town of Lambertville) in the 1700s from the Delaware Indians. Is it possible this piece of land the high school sits on is cursed?

Two legends are associated with Lambertville High School. If you stand on the landing between the first and the second floor near the doors and say aloud the phrase, "I challenge the Buckeyes to a football game!", out of nowhere a football will be flying straight towards your head, attempting to break your neck. The second legend allegedly takes place on the football field itself. If you say aloud the phrase, "Buckeyes, I challenge you to a race!", suddenly the wind will start to gently blow. A mist then starts to form and you will see a pair of glowing red eyes appearing at one end of the field and a voice will say, "Run to the other end of the field — or die!"

It has been also said that kids have been known to commit suicide by jumping out of a third floor window in the area where the gym is located, possibly related to one of the fires that had taken place in past years. Some versions of the legend vary as to a girl by the name of Maria, who was involved with one of two boys. Not an official sporting event, the two boys were engaged in a race, the winner winning the girl's affection; however, one of the boys died as a result of the race.

We are sure that there must be some truth to the boy's death as many a school athlete or even a professional athlete has been injured or disabled during a game, accounts of which have been published in newspapers across the country for decades. Sometimes a legend is worth investigating, which can lead to a ghost story and perhaps an actual haunting captured on camera, video, or even audio recorder. This was our intent when we set out to see if we could experience something paranormal or to at least see if there is some truth to the legend. Many people have made the pilgrimage and experienced something or have gotten something paranormal in nature when photographing at the Lambertville High School and no doubt many a teenager trespassing.

After doing a little research, it was deemed trespasser risky, largely due to a housing development that you need to pass through in order to reach the base of the hill that the high school sits on. This fact, coupled with the decaying condition of the structure, made us decide that we would go with the intent of photographing and seeing if doing some EVP sessions was feasible. We also looked online to see if we could find any newspaper articles, but it was not clear what year this supposed football game or subsequent accident took place, so to-date our investigation remains incomplete.

Chapter 23

Secrets of the 'Lodge on the Lake'

We had absolutely no idea what to expect when we agreed to investigate this particular location. I don't even know how I knew that this place was rumored to be "haunted." The building wasn't an old building, maybe seventy plus years old. Nevertheless, after hearing claims of "paranormal" experiences from some of the members who belong to this lodge, it certainly was worth it to go there. If anything, the building sounded interesting. As you drove down the long road, nestled in the woods on the edge of town, it seemed a little intriguing, especially after dark. The lake behind the lodge only added to the atmosphere this building seemed to be taking on. The building's design wasn't much to look at. It wasn't rife with spectacular architecture and, as matter of fact, it seemed fairly plain. If you didn't know the area, you would have no idea this building existed except for the modest sign. You wouldn't guess there was a huge lake either and, of course, the word "investigation" is always welcome.

General view of "Haunted" lodge.

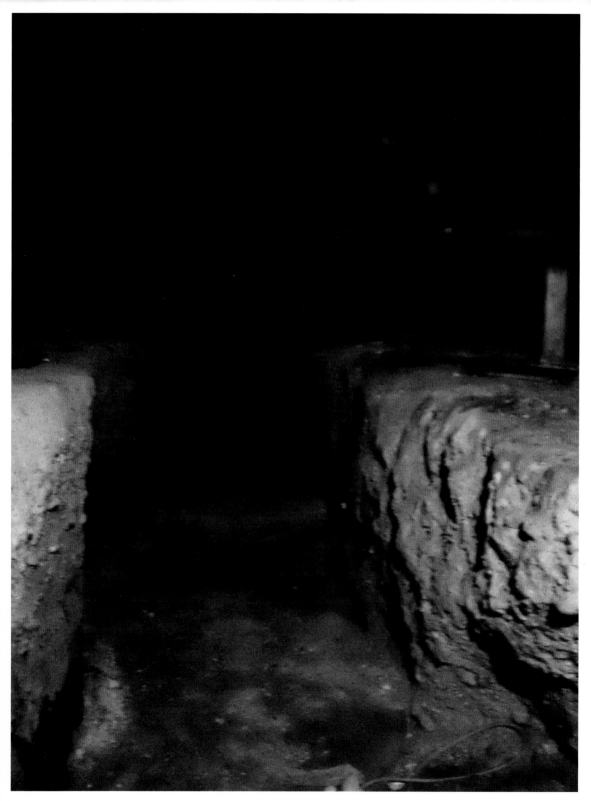

Tunnels beneath the lodge.

Once inside the lodge, you get the feeling you are trapped inside a "Nancy Drew" mystery novel. The hidden staircase is one of the first things you will come across—or will you? It's disguised pretty well to blend in with the matching coat room's door. Once beyond the foyer you are in the "lodge." It has a bar area and bookcases. One of the bookcases turns and you can go through to the kitchens. Downstairs is a room they call "The Ship Room." You walk in and you feel like you are on a ship. There are "windows" that once doubled as fish tanks; I suppose to make you feel like you are under the sea. There is also a ship's mast that travels through all of the floors and ceilings. The floor at one time supported springs, so when you walked on the floor you had to get your sea legs working, to make you feel like you were on a real ship. On one of the walls hung a portrait of a man wearing a ship captain's hat. Oh, did I mention the tunnels that go out to the lake? Sounds a little weird, right? All of these eccentricities started to make a little more sense as we found out the history.

Ahoy Mate

To give you a better understanding of this story, the Nixon family owned the property before selling it to the B.P.O.E. The elder Nixon was Lewis Nixon, a Naval Architect, political activist, industrialist, and owner of the Nixon Nitration Works facilities on the Raritan River, near New Brunswick, now where Middlesex County College and the Raritan Arsenal is, hence the "Navy theme" throughout the Ship Room. He was the father of Stanhope and the grandfather of his namesake Lewis, who was an officer in the 101st Airborne Division during Word War II that was made famous by the miniseries *Band of Brothers*; Lewis, the grandson, died in 1995.

The elder Nixon founded Nixon Nitration Works in 1915 at the outbreak of World War I to supply some of the warring European nations with gunpowder and other materials. When the war was over, Nixon Nitration's facilities were put to broader use involving other explosive materials. One of the materials being manufactured was cellulose nitrate. A precursor to plastic, the material was highly flammable and it was being stored in buildings on the property. Because the plant was near the Raritan Arsenal's property, it was speculated that materials from the company Ammonite and what was being stored by Nixon Nitration, as well as possible poor conditions at either company's facilities, created the explosive disaster that killed at least thirty people. Windows and doors for miles around the area were damaged and ripped off their hinges. The blast shook Staten Island and was heard as far away as New York City. When the elder Nixon passed away in 1940 (he had lived in New Brunswick with his wife Sally who passed away in 1937), his son Stanhope assumed control of the business. Stanhope was different than his father, but had many vices.

Keeping your balance in the Ships Room located on the lower
level of the lodge may prove an interesting experience.

When we checked township records, many buildings sat on the lodge's property, some no doubt from the original farmland and some that still sit abandoned. One of the boathouses on the property had burned down at one point. Most were demolished in 1974 when the B.P.O.E. purchased them. The property includes the house, built in 1903, but more was added in 1937 to include guest housing, apartments and garage, an in-ground pool, and the lodge. It would appear that the Nixon family owned the property at this point through Stanhope, who took over the business. We have been told that the lodge was used for entertainment, which included sneaking women in and out, parties, and bootlegging activities. With the lake right there and tunnels underground, it made these activities seem all too real. The Ship Room made sense now as well. It was a tribute to the elder Nixon. Rumors have it that at one time the portrait of Nixon was removed or discarded and it wasn't long after that it was anonymously returned to the lodge because of either bad vibes coming from the portrait or a bad experience.

The Investigation

We went into the investigation hearing of lodge members' experiences of possible "paranormal activity," some of which included doors slamming and seeing the apparitions of a Civil War soldier, a little girl, a woman, and a cat. Both the girl and the cat were seen and heard on occasions. At times the girl seemed to be asking where her ball was. She seemed so real that one night, after a lodge member locked up and was driving down the long road leading out, he saw a child in the road in their rearview mirror. The police were called to see if anyone reported a child missing. The caretaker for the lodge who resides in the front house reports similar sightings both at the lodge and the house. The inhabitants of the house also reported having headaches and sleep disturbances. This explains the high electromagnetism recorded on our EMF detectors, which we found could be the house's wiring coming through the middle of the house. This could be the cause of the headaches, sleep disturbances, and shadows seen by the caretaker. However, it doesn't explain the experiences of lodge members or the caretaker at the lodge building.

In both the lodge and the house, our psychic picked up on numerous spirits. She sees the soldier walking the hall of the house on the side where guest housing once was. She also sees him in the lodge. It would make sense; he no doubt was there when the property was just farmland. This is exactly what she feels. Many spirits are attached to the land. When the psychic and I entered an area of the house with the most reported activity, we both heard a distinctive "breath." Our other psychic saw the child sitting on the back porch of the house. She had no prior knowledge of this location, its history, or reported activity. The first psychic, on the other hand, had a little knowledge of the location, as she is a member of the B.P.O.E.

We decided that because the psychics were picking up on numerous spirits we would have a séance to see if we could identify some of them directly with the lodge. The names "Thomas," "John," "Michael," and "Irv" — even though they are common names — kept coming up during the séance. "John" was here in the 1970s and died of a heart attack. We couldn't confirm this. Both psychics saw the cat. Some of the team kept feeling something hugging their ankles. One psychic's hair was touched on a couple of occasions. Some of the female names mentioned during the séance were "Abigail" and "Mary," again, common names. By asking certain questions, we got another year "1843." Whenever there was a mention of the coldness and movement around some of the team member's ankles, there would be a spike in the EMF detector. At one point, the line of questioning produced an energy that was felt by several members of the team and one of the psychics felt strong chills just prior to the surge in energy. When we thanked the spirits, the EMF detector spiked again, the room got cold, and the candles flickered. After the team had gone, loud raps were heard coming from the room. We left these investigations, of both the lodge and the house (we investigated the house on the eve of Halloween), with the feeling that there is more to be discovered here.

Soon after, NJGO began having its annual PARA-X at the lodge. PARA-X is a Paranormal Expo that the organization initiated; it's designed to introduce to the public what the paranormal field does. The theme can change from year to year. At last year's expo, I was giving a tour to one of the local artists who participated. We were down in the tunnels and I took him to see the Ship Room. As soon as we talked about getting back upstairs to the expo, the door — not the Ship Room's door but the door just beyond it — slammed shut. Now, neither of us scares very easily, and I, being an investigator, naturally gravitated quickly to the source and went over to that door. We tried and tested the door and could not find a mechanical reason why the door would slam so abruptly. The door to the upstairs main floor had not been touched and remained closed, so no vacuum was created making this downstairs door react. Apparently, someone did not want us to leave.

The Analysis

We were somewhat satisfied that we at least got to experience some of the claims reported to us and which over time have been experienced by both lodge members and the caretaker. We captured on camera a very low density orb in the room where we conducted the séance, as well as video showing a higher density, more self-luminous orb moving very low to the ground near one of the psychics. At the time, she was heading toward one of the team members who experienced coldness and movement around their ankles. Could this have been the "cat" both psychics saw and lodge members reported seeing and hearing? It's a good possibility. Was "John," who one of our psychics mentioned had a heart attack in the 1970s, involved with the demolition of the buildings on the property in 1974? We have a record of paperwork showing which buildings were torn down in 1974 when we followed up with some research following the investigation.

Every piece of property has a history — maybe not the type of history that makes us curious, but a history nonetheless. Any type of event, whether tragic or not, can leave an imprint that enables us to experience something. In this particular investigation, the numerous spirits picked up on by the psychics could very well be from many different time periods. Some can be residual, some active to the point where the psychics are receiving bits of information from them, or, in the case of the cat, members physically feeling the cat. The child seems residual; although the psychic saw "her" on the back porch and, while "she" was out on the road, "she" doesn't really leave the area. The caretaker has heard her and the child has said, "Have you seen my ball?" She's an active spirit, most likely trapped here until she finds her ball.

Because of what the building is used for currently, a lodge where members are constantly in and out, it's hard to pinpoint specific times these experiences are occurring and if they are, in fact, repeating at these specific times. It does not seem so, as we would agree these would be mostly active, intelligent spirits attempting to communicate and make noise. We also captured on video a bright, pulsating energy that seemed to be reacting to the stronger line of questioning during the séance. Was it agitated? It didn't seem like we were communicating with anyone from the Nixon family, who have probably moved on since it's likely that New Jersey holds a lot of bad memories for them and their connection with the Nitration disaster. Still, there are plenty of other souls who are here.

Chapter 24

Fire and Water

The town of Mount Holly is no stranger to local folklore. We were given this fantastic opportunity to follow-up on some of the tales we were hearing on several of our visits to Mount Holly, including being able to investigate the oldest, continuous operating volunteer firehouse in the country.

One of the local tales is that of a fire that had taken place next-door to where the original part of the firehouse is located today. This scenario would have been back in the early to mid-1700s. It was unclear if this fire had first taken place where the newer part of the firehouse was added or on the next lot over from the old structure. It's also unclear where the original building sits. Either way, our psychic felt that there was a family whose house horrifically burned down. She said there were seven children, two of whom died. Is this why we were privy to the number five during an EVP session? We kept asking, how many of you are here? We asked if they were men, women, or children and we were receiving a strong reading on our KII meter when asking about children. When we mentioned one at a time to determine just how many children were here with us, we skipped over some. One? Two? We then skipped over three, four, and five...going directly to the number seven. When we played back our voice recorder after our trip to the firehouse, the reply was five.

Could it be that five little girls are still roaming the grounds? One of the images that we were fortunate to have captured on camera was what appears to be a child-size shadow on the wall at the top of a staircase appearing to be wearing a child-size fire helmet. Still, one question begs for an answer: What happened to the other two children who had allegedly died in the fire? Our psychic had seen seven children. Was the local story true that children did perish in a house fire adjacent to the firehouse? Both of these stories may forever remain a mystery.

From the moment we arrived our psychic had a very uncomfortable feeling when on the ground floor. She is relaying that something happened and that she needed to go two blocks down from the firehouse and to the right. Well, it was late in the evening and at that point this was not an option with a night of investigation barely beginning. A local fireman later recalled that a drowning had taken place two blocks from the firehouse; a stream was involved and a girl drowned approximately six or seven years ago. What our psychic was receiving was perhaps a murder, but it had something to do with drowning and a bridge or near a bridge.

Staircase apparition is reflected in the mirror.

Either an unknown male person did something unknowingly that caused the outcome or did not try and prevent the outcome. Psychic impressions revealed that the girl's death was ruled a suicide or accidental death, a point that was never really clear. The spirit that our psychic was seeing was telling her that it was not on purpose and "to please tell my sister." Apparently this spirit was not going to let go, now that she was able to make contact, until she told her story.

We had never investigated a firehouse before, so how do we handle this? It hasn't been shut down — it was a working, operating, active firehouse. We thought about it and came to the conclusion that not only does adrenaline run high at a firehouse, but also emotions. You return from a fire call after someone perishes in a fire, maybe you tried to save that person or save his or her property. It is very possible that you could capture that latent, or leftover, energy with your equipment. They actually have the "original" building on the premises, which looked like an outhouse, but we knew back in the 1700s, before actual fire trucks like we see today they had what's called pumpers and that's exactly what they did! The pumper was horse-drawn and carried water. The water was pumped into leather buckets, so many of which had to be used that they had an "outhouse" to store the buckets and probably food for the horses.

Built in 1752, the now town of Mount Holly, New Jersey, a very impressive 250 years later, we were about to see this firehouse still standing in all of its past glory. The original structure is attached to the newer truck bays. In an effort to preserve this treasure, when they added the newer bays, they only broke through a small section of the older house, thus joining both structures to accommodate all of their trucks. When entering the older half, it is like taking a step back in time. From the outside, the building is very tall and overshadowing when looking up at this magnificent structure and architecture. It has a bell tower with gingerbread style trim work. When you step inside, the windows, the trim, the wood is all original, as well as some of the remnants of an era long gone. As you ascend the staircase, the same ones the firemen who are no longer with us ran up and down, you can feel the rich history. The top floor boasts three rooms, each one larger than the next. The crown jewel is their meeting room. Sectioned off by the very large wooden panels as if you would be entering a grand ballroom, the first thing you notice is how big the room is. The old copper-painted ceiling containing a few very large chandeliers still remains, adding to the mystique of the moment. Next, you cannot help but to take notice of a few dozen wooden chairs lining the walls in the same position as they were back during the 1700s. This room is where many firemen have gathered for centuries, volunteering their time, risking their lives, saving lives and property at a moment's notice. There are many antiques safely tucked away in a large floor to ceiling glass cabinet, which gives you an eerie feeling. In this case were actual items belonging to people who are no longer here, fire buckets that were passed down the line from man to man in an effort to save someone's burning home, uniforms worn by an unknown hero, badges, bugles, lanterns, and more. It is a lot to take in, however, from such a primitive era in time. It was not the technology and tools that we have today to fight fires, but to know that these men fought bravely and at the same time it is a comfort to those who understand the meaning of a brotherhood and to preserve something so important for generations to come, see, and touch that affords us this opportunity. Even though these men (and women) are still volunteers like many across the United States, they abide by rules and are a working organization, like a well-oiled machine. When one man should perish, it not only affects their family — it affects a whole community. That is a very tough act to follow!

The Investigation

We begin our investigation into the unknown once again. Will we capture a voice from the past, a lingering spirit, and a fireman who knows this building as his only home and its members as his family? We can only hope so.

When we spoke to representatives from the fire company, we had an idea of the types of experiences they were having: paranormal experiences and unexplained phenomenon. Fire coats moving as they hung on their respective hooks on the wall as if someone or something walked past them and ran their hand across each coat—or maybe it was one of the Dalmatian dogs running through to make the truck and its tail was hitting the coats? After all, one of the company's firedogs died in the line of duty — he died of a heart attack climbing onto the truck to answer a fire call. One fireman mentioned that members would go into the meeting room to find, on several occasions, one of the chairs in the middle of the floor, not against the wall like all of the rest. This particular chair a past fireman claimed very adamantly as his every time he was in the building.

At the time, it seemed the most advantageous to concentrate on the upper floor mostly because this was a working firehouse. Our decision paid off because we were able to get some evidence to show them. In a case such as this, it was best to focus on just a couple of areas and not roam the entire building. We took the time to set up our equipment and immediately began to use our voice recorders to attempt to engage in a conversation with the other side. We brought along one of our group's psychics in an effort to support any evidence we may get. The evening was off to a good start. As the night progressed, some of the team and fire personnel did have some personal experiences, feeling as though something was behind you and a tug or touch. These types of experiences don't happen frequently, but they do happen. In the end, the evidence speaks for itself.

We capped the evening with a séance with our KII meters (electromagnetic field detectors) on and got several strong hits while asking questions. Our personal feeling is because of what makes these detectors register is the basic concept of an interruption in an electromagnetic field, energy is interrupting energy and the KII meters are quicker to pick this up. In our case spirit energy is crossing this field. It would seem as though the spirit is using energy to interact with the KII meter. We had already had major battery drains on some of the equipment throughout the evening for an unexplained reason.

A few of the highlights included trying to establish exactly how many spirits were there with us. The psychic was receiving the number "7" throughout most of the night. We asked in succession one? Two? and so on. We got up to the number seven and seeing that there was a delay on the KII meter we thought seven to be the correct number; however, there still remained some doubt. When we reviewed the digital voice recorder right before this, you can just barely hear the number five being spoken. We believe the spirit was correcting us. We asked the question, "Can you see us?" The KII meter lit up undeniably…it was yes.

The Analysis

After reviewing all of what we think is potential evidence, we were left with three important photos. The first was what appears to be a figure standing on the stairs with what looks like a fire helmet on. It was obvious to us that it was a child. In the second photo, a different team's photographer captured a figure over by one of the chairs and the third series of photos was that of our psychic. Questions were being asked if "anyone" here with us had an attachment to anything in the glass case. The psychic experienced a cold chill and saw what appeared to be a large dark mass, which would be behind her opposite the glass case. When she got the chill and saw the dark mass out of the corner of her eye, she turned around and took a succession of photos. The mass appeared in the photos, slowly getting darker.

It seems plausible that there are a couple of things occurring here. Latent energy is a possibility, but that was ruled out. It had active spirits dropping in or visiting — this is what we believe we experienced on our visit. It was interesting because the thought occurred that it would seem more likely we could very well capture evidence of a residual haunting, some repetition, something leftover because of emotions running high due to the nature of the business. The dark mass appears to be associated with the chill and the reference by the psychic of a possible attachment to someone's equipment in the glass cabinet is a reaction, not something being repetitious associated with something residual. Was the child returning? Or maybe it never left because it may have been a happier moment in their life or they like it there? Lots of kids each year will tell you, 'I want to be a fireman when I grow up.' Weighing in everything — personal experiences, the photos, the documentation of the hits on the KII to specific questions, and a voice on the recorder — the firehouse definitely fits the paranormal field's definition of "active." Not only that, but it is continuous in its operations and the oldest in the United States.

Do the men and women of the firehouse tell tales of bygone days, repeating ones that have been passed down through the centuries? They most certainly do, as does the older generations of townsfolk, but you must visit here yourself. I am certain that you will walk away with both fact and, yes, a bit of fiction to add to the annals of folklore.

Chapter 25

The Black Butterfly

Presidential Royalty in New Jersey

Back in the 1700s two brothers by the name of Mordecai and Abraham migrated to Monmouth County and operated a blacksmith shop. Mordecai met and married a woman by the name of Hannah Salter, a wealthy mill owner's daughter. Why is this so important? Because the brother's last name was Lincoln — and Mordecai and Hannah became the great-great-grandparents of our 16th President of the United States of America, Abraham Lincoln.

One of the many children Mordecai and Hannah had was a girl named Deborah Lincoln. Unfortunately little Deborah died on May 15, 1720, at the age of three. She would never know she would become the great-grand aunt to one of our nation's most influential leaders. With no real place to bury Deborah, it was decided she would remain in New Jersey for all of eternity,

as the Lincolns left New Jersey and after moving around several times finally settled in Kentucky where our future President was born in 1809.

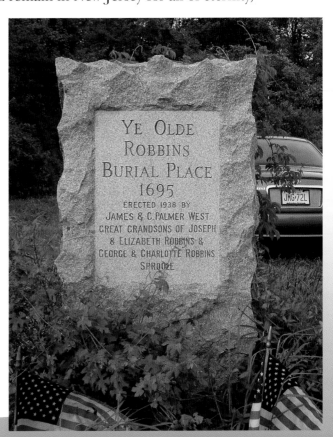

Robinsville Cemetery memorial near entrance.

Off the Beaten Path

The cemetery, established in 1695, belonged to the Robbins Family and I believe it was originally intended for the family. It is barely visible from the road; however, after navigating the winding path up a steep hill, many final resting places will come into view. Some of the resting places were once decorated with ornate iron fences, but have since succumbed to weather and time. Some were fallen and hidden by the thick ground brush, a very surprising sight to behold.

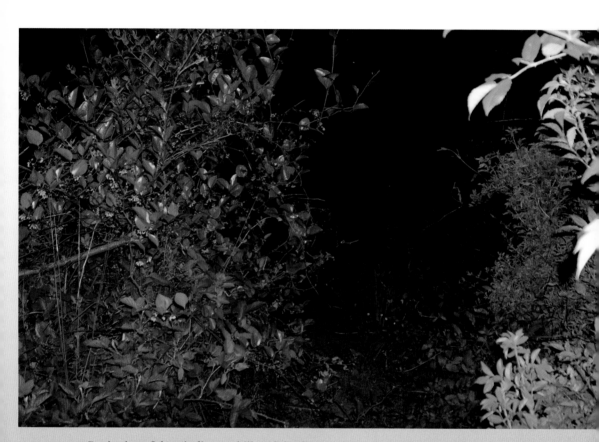

Beginning of the winding up hill path leading to the cemetery proper.

Little Deborah's gravestone sits alone behind an iron fence. Her stone is not the type of headstone you would know today. It's a stone indigenous to the type of New Jersey rock, red sandstone, but hand-chiseled. It reads: "Deborah Lincoln Aged 3 years 4 months May 15, 1720." I have read many stories of ghostly claims, from folks hearing horse and carriages ascending on the cemetery to ghostly cries, especially happening on the anniversary of little Deborah's death.

Inundating the immediate area of the cemetery are "Black Butterflies" and the locals who venture up the winding path say that these are not seen anywhere else in the area. When we visited the area near the gravesite of Deborah, one of the black butterflies seemed to be lingering and landed on one of our team member's finger, remaining there for quite a long time. One of our psychics had the feeling it was a spirit. Should this be the case, then visiting the cemetery may just satisfy your curiosity.

General view inside cemetery.

Deborah Lincoln's gravesite.

The Analysis

Yes, we skipped the investigation. My belief and experience in cemeteries is simple. Any potential evidence risks the chance of being contaminated simply because you are working outdoors. The team spent a spring evening, leaving the narrow path illuminated with glow sticks so we could find our way back down later on. The cemetery was so eerily still you would probably hear a pin drop. We set up both video cameras and digital voice recorders and began taking still digital photos. You might wonder why would there be any activity in a cemetery; after all, if I were dead, would I hang around my grave? Would you?

We did explore all of the graves to see who was buried there and it was very interesting. Many of those buried there are entire families and Civil War veterans. We did not get to experience any of the written about claims of ghostly sounds. It would seem like those buried could be at peace and have moved on. After all, some of the oldest burials occurred starting about 315 years ago and none were buried in the twenty-first century or even back to the twentieth century that we could see. One of our photographer's did get a couple of orbs on video camera later on after it became really dark into the evening.

It makes you sad when you think about it that little Deborah rests alone with no family nearby or that her relatives did not come to take her body back to perhaps Kentucky. At least she has compassionate strangers that come to pay their respects every now and again.

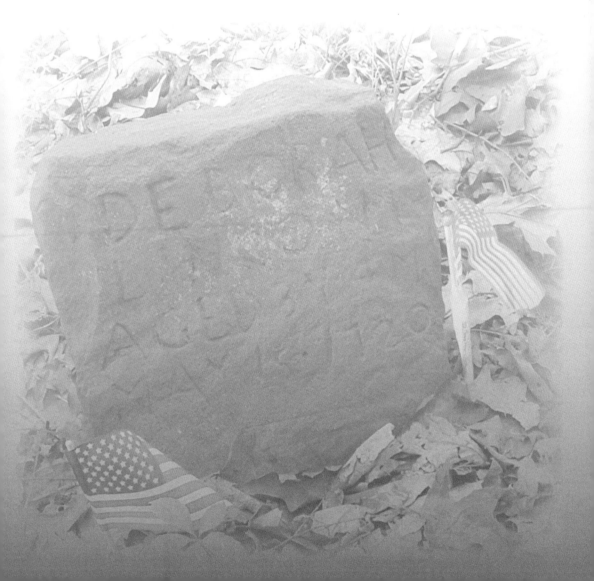

Chapter 26

Folk-bits

Emily

Hotel employees and guests have very often and openly told the story of the Lady in White that they claim to see at the Flanders Hotel in Ocean City, New Jersey. The locals know of her only as Emily, but, in fact, nobody knows her real name. There are no photographs of Emily, but she is described as having long brownish or auburn hair, a long white dress, barefoot, and appears to be in her early twenties.

Another tale of Emily is that she roams this Ocean City beach waiting for her husband to return from war. No one is sure if that is World War One or World War Two. This boardwalk hotel was built in the early 1900s and the locals feel that Emily roams the hotel and beach and could be from a completely different era even before the Flanders was built.

Dempsey House, Leonardo, New Jersey

Mr. Dempsey was said to be sick, an older gentleman who was unable to get out of bed and depended on his wife to take care of him. One day she went out somewhere and for some reason she never came back. So Mr. Dempsey just lay upstairs alone until he died. Soon after, one of the neighbors called the police, probably because of the smell of a rotting body. The officer entered the house and a few minutes later he came back outside and hanged himself on a tree. No one ever knew why because he never said anything… he just killed himself. Now, this would seem pretty bizarre until you walk across the street where you will notice a rope dangling from a tree.

In contrast to this, some say that Mr. Dempsey lived in the house with his wife and three kids and one night he went insane, killed them all, burned the bodies in the three boilers that were down in the basement, and then took his own life. Should you enter the basement, you may see something run across it. If you do, leave as fast as you can and do not look back.

Unfortunately, all that remains of the old Dempsey estate in the Leonardo section of Middletown is a rustic pump house.

"Haunting" skull on wooden post.

Ancora's Village of the Damned

Near New Jersey's western shore area is a town called Ancora that is completely abandoned, an entire development of bungalow type houses. Nobody really knows what happened, but the folklore surrounding it indicates that there had been an escapee from the mental hospital across the road and he murdered as many as seventy people one night. Driving through the town, you will experience a very weird feeling as you notice that in some of the houses there is still furniture with cars in their driveways. The town is adjacent to the Ancora Psychiatric Hospital housing the criminally insane, just outside the towns of Atco and Hammonton. The town is slowly being demolished, but what will remain afterward?

Strange lights in Double Trouble Park – Folklore Or?

Double Trouble Park is located on the Cedar Creek in Berkley Township, Ocean County. Strange lights have been seen coming from the area. The FAA thought a plane went down there, but could never find any traces.

The unusual thing is that whatever landed there pushed the trees down so flat, yet did not destroy them. The dimensions are pretty large and form a complete circle. It is a very creepy area and if you have a digital watch, compass, or take a photograph the flattened circular area will not show in the picture and your watch or compass will go crazy!

Entrance sign to Double Trouble Park.

Ocean Grove

Ocean Grove, just a stone's through from Asbury Park, is an unincorporated community in Neptune Township, Monmouth County, New Jersey. It is located on the Jersey Shore, between Asbury Park to the north and Bradley Beach to the south. Listed on the National Register of Historic Places, Ocean Grove is noted for its abundant examples of Victorian architecture.

Ocean Grove was founded in 1869 as an outgrowth of the camp meeting movement in the United States, when a group of Methodist clergymen, led by William B. Osborne and Ellwood H. Stokes, formed the Ocean Grove Camp Meeting Association to develop and operate a summer camp meeting site on the New Jersey seashore. By the early twentieth century, the popular Christian meeting ground became known as the "Queen of Religious Resorts." The community's land is still owned by the camp meeting association and leased to individual homeowners and businesses. Ocean Grove remains the longest-active camp meeting site in the United States.

Asbury Park has become synonymous with this famous summer resort town, though there is nothing atypical regarding Ocean Grove, New Jersey, during the day. However, this is a city where it is said that the undead of days gone by walk the avenues in the moonlight hours. Some of the dead in this settlement will not crossover. As legend would have it, people who live here argue there are no ghosts, but seeing is believing — and if you spend the night here in Ocean Grove, you may catch a glimpse of a ghost.

General view inside park.

General view inside park.

Avon By The Sea

Although many of the vacationers and locals call it Avon, the correct pronunciation is Ah-von. At this quaint Victorian seaside resort town, both the locals and visitors claim that during the daylight hours Avon By The Sea is like any other municipality, but when the darkness of night commences things become terrifying. Unusual things begin to happen in some of the seaside cottages, screams coming out of the darkness. Not everybody believes in the descriptions the people who live here tell, but bloodcurdling things undeniably go down here in Avon By The Sea during the dark of night.

Belmar's Beach

What is now Belmar, New Jersey, was originally incorporated as Ocean Beach Borough on April 9, 1885, from portions of Wall Township. On April 16, 1889, it became the City of Elcho Borough, which lasted for a few weeks until the name was changed to the City of Belmar Borough as of May 14, 1889. The city acquired its current name, Borough of Belmar, on November 20, 1890.

The locals claim that there are times when the beach is deserted, looking out to sea, you may see a clear outline of a ship between the jetty and the ocean — so clear that you can actually count the number of unfurled masts and the positions of things on deck. Most often, when you begin to walk away and return a quick glance, the ship seems to have slowly dissolved into thin air.

Lenni-Lenape Indians Still on the Shore Trails

The Lenape people occupied the Tuckerton area long before European colonists settled here. They spent summers at the Jersey Shore feasting on fish, clams, oysters, and mussels, also hunting game in the summer. Locals claim that when walking some of the ocean trails or just being on one of the beaches during the summer months, especially at sunset, one of the tribe may pass you…still walking in residual silence from a time long passed into the annals of New Jersey's history.

Angel of the Sea Forever More

Willing Weightman of Philadelphia, Pennsylvania, built this seashore bed and breakfast located in Cape May in 1850. Eventually the home's location was moved twice in the 1960s from its original location in two sections, later to be joined into one. Some locals say that the house had to be moved in two pieces, as it possibly had split apart when first attempting to move it and could not be seamlessly attached, becoming the largest bed and breakfast you will see in Cape May.

In the late 1960s, the Angel was used as a dormitory for the housing of employees of the Christian Admiral Hotel and for a few other places in the area. The tale is told about a young employee of the Christian Admiral who was returning to her room at the Angel after finishing her shift and, realizing that she was without her keys, thought that perhaps she could exit through a hallway window and climb out onto the ledge to the adjoined part of the Angel to her room window. Upon reaching the ledge of her window, she found that the screen was stuck shut. When she was finally able to free the screen, it sent her to her death on the ground below. She is said to have died between the two buildings and it seems that ever since, doors in the Angel tend to lock and unlock by themselves and electrical objects are disrupted.

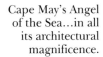

Cape May's Angel of the Sea...in all its architectural magnificence.

No a Stranger to Folktales

Point Pleasant, New Jersey, has had its share of tales and one that is told frequently is connected to the Fireside Inn. Reportedly, the Fireside Inn is the oldest inn in New Jersey and was at one time operated as a stagecoach stop as far back as the 1800s and as a bordello in the 1920s. Abuse and death is believed to be associated with the inn, specifically of a caretaker who died of a head injury from one of the horses during the time that the inn was a stagecoach stopping point.

The Exit "82" Phantom

In a section of the Garden State Parkway, in the shore area, passing motorists tell a story that a spectral man appears at nightfall, seemingly to be crossing the roadway. This particular stretch of the GSP is reported to have a particularly high count of accidents. Is this spectral phantom simply warning drivers to slow down and use caution? Well, should you ever see him, you be the judge!

Elephant's Watery Grave

An elephant buried at sea? Local lore claims that an elephant traveling with the Ringling Brother's Circus back in the early 1900s became a danger during the Circus in Europe and had to be euthanized. As the story is told, the elephant was placed into a crate, later to be disposed of in the ocean. When the ship arrived in New York Harbor, a tugboat transported the elephant's lifeless body to nearby Sandy Hook, New Jersey, where it was remanded to the sea.

Parkway Tombstone

Along the Garden State Parkway in Cape May County, resting in peace, is the gravesite of Noah Cherry, a Civil War veteran who passed away in 1907. Originally a slave, it is presumed that he died a free man and you may pay your respects to him in the southbound lane around mile marker 16. Rumor has it that at times passersby have seen a figure of an individual wearing some sort of uniform standing near the tombstone, but none have yet to muster the nerve to pull to the side of the road to take a closer look. This is what the alleged figure may wish someone to do, but would it be safe?

Martians at Grover's Mill

Orson Wells and his famous radio broadcast an episode of the American radio drama anthology series "Mercury Theater on the Air" that was performed as a Halloween episode on October 30, 1938, and aired over the Columbia Broadcasting System radio network. Directed and narrated by actor and filmmaker Orson Wells, the episode was an adaptation of H.G. Wells' novel *The War of the Worlds*.

The first part of the broadcast was a series of simulated news bulletins suggesting that an actual alien invasion by Martians was in progress. Compounding this was the fact that "Mercury Theater on the Air" was a 'sustaining show' (a show running without commercial breaks), thus adding to the program's quality of realism. This was a volatile combination causing sensationalist accounts in the press about a supposed panic in response to the broadcast of which the exact extent of the listener response has been a topic of debate then and, in some circles, may still be today.

However, in the days following the adaptation, there was widespread outrage and panic by those who believed that the events described in the program were actually real. The news-bulletin format of the program was decried as being cruelly deceptive by a few newspapers and some public figures and led to an outcry against the perpetrators of the broadcast, but the episode secured Orson Wells' future fame.

As the plot of this scenario thickens, news grows more frequent and increasingly ominous as a cylindrical meteorite lands in Grover's Mill, New Jersey. Reporter Carl Phillips relates events as a crowd gathers at the site; to onlookers the meteorite unscrews, revealing itself as a rocket machine, catching a glimpse of a tentacled, pulsating, barely mobile Martian before incinerating the crowd with heat-rays. Phillips' excited shouts about the incoming flames are cut-off in mid-sentence. Some later surveys indicated that many of the listeners had only heard this portion of the show before making frantic calls to neighbors or family members who were inquiring about the broadcast. Thus began an unbridled series of contacts, leading to rumors and confusion.

Even today this story is on the lips of the locals and is carried away by visitors to the area. These tales of little green men roaming the area and alien spacecraft heading eastward toward the Jersey seashore coastal area foster more tales of the spacecraft entering the oceans' depths.

The Graveyard Inlet in Absecon

In one nasty two-month period — December 1826 to January 1827 — two hundred wrecks took place along Absecon Island (now Atlantic City). Lighthouses helped, but more was needed. The Absecon inlet is home to the Absecon Lighthouse. Sitting near the Marina in Atlantic City is the tallest of the New Jersey Lighthouses at an impressive 171 feet tall and 228 steps to the light's tower. Built in 1857 and decommissioned in 1933, the lighthouse no longer serves navigationally; however, the light has remained lit for the past 154 years, but not without seeing tragedy.

In 1905, one of the earlier lightkeepers claims to have seen the New Jersey Devil atop the lighthouse tower and then vanish. The lighthouse has also seen its share of tragedy, as was the case on July 6, 1998. A massive fire destroyed the lightkeeper's home, luckily the tower came through completely unscathed and no one was injured. Unfortunately, over the years, there were seven deaths that occurred in the keeper's house. In April 1854, it garnered the nickname "graveyard inlet" with a shipwreck off its coast: the *Owatonna* lost all 311 passengers and crew.

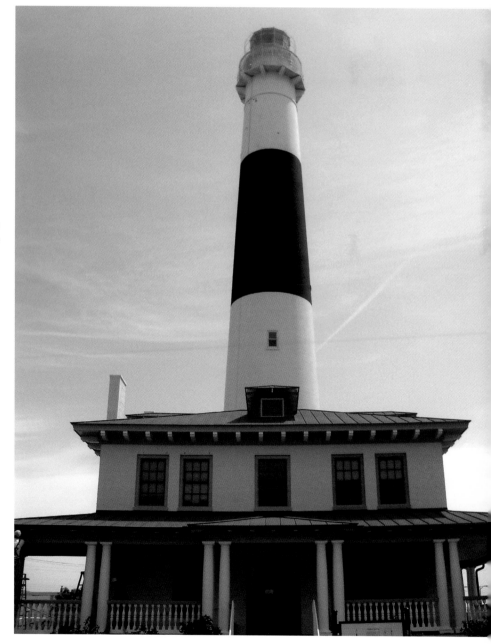

Absecon Lighthouse.

There have been numerous claims of visitors smelling pipe tobacco and seeing apparitions roaming the lighthouse. Do the previous lightkeepers still roam the property in which they've been responsible for so long? Do the passengers and crew of the *Owatonna* remain in watery graves for their final unrest?

How "Wild" Is Wildwood

Does Wildwood really live up to its name? If you are considering UFO activity, you may be right, as many stories have emanated from this New Jersey Shore retreat.

Wildwood's beginnings stem from the English Navigator Henry Hudson and a voyage in 1609 seeking a new route to China. Upon entering the Delaware Bay on August 28, 1609, he quickly turned around after realizing that the inlet he and his crew had sailed into was not the Northwest Passage. After exploring the inlet, Hudson and his voyagers watched contently upon their boat the *Half Moon* as the waves broke across the beautiful 1.8-mile stretch of beach, now known as the Five Mile Beach. Some say that you may still see the *Half Moon* on the anniversary date of this mistaken voyage.

Now, back to the stories of little green men alleged to be seen prancing about on the beach or peering out from under the boardwalk — true or not, one can never be certain; at least as stories go!

Magnificent aerial view of
Wildwood, New Jersey.

Cape May's Spirited Folklore

At the terminus of the Garden State Parkway in New Jersey is the charming Victorian-themed resort town of Cape May, a town that was at one time known as Cape Island City. The town bustles during the summer months and was the premier resort for Philadelphians who wanted to escape the steamy hot summers of the big city.

The remodeling of old buildings foster many stories of hauntings and claims of resident ghosts not being violent or threatening, but were instead given names by the homeowners in a fond, lighthearted way. "Oh, have you met Esmeralda, the ghost of a nanny who once lived here?" Qualities bestowed on Esmeralda were passed on in the stories to visitors and guests.

In 1766, the Scow *Nancy* was lost along the Cape May coastline in a violent gale. Witnesses watched in horror as twenty-three souls lost their lives. The Jersey Shore was littered with shipwrecks; some caused by storms and accidents, but many were caused intentionally by wreckers. The story of an old trick was to hang a lantern from a mule's neck and to walk the beast back and forth along the shoreline on a dark, stormy night. An unfortunate captain who lost his bearings would think the light was from another vessel, a safe distance from shore, and would suddenly find his vessel snagged on a deadly shoal. "Pickens" filled many a seaside homestead or inn and there were even reports of locals refusing to provide assistance and rifling through bodies as they came to rest on the beach. Late at night, ships passing this area claim to see a light moving along the shoreline... Could this be the legendary "mule" still walking his light?

A Gem from Days Gone By

Lakewood, New Jersey's Strand Theater was built for the Ferber Amusement Company in 1922 by Thomas W. Lamb to serve as a try-out venue for Broadway shows before they actually went to Broadway in 1922. However, within a couple years of its opening, the Strand Theatre began to host vaudeville shows and silent films, as well as the occasional play or musical. Among the stars that appeared on the Strand's stage early in their careers were Burns & Allen, Milton Berle, and Ray Bolger.

By the end of the 1940s, the Strand Theater was only showing films. The theater closed in the late 1970s, unable to compete with television and nearby suburban mall theaters. In 1981, the vacant but still intact Strand Theatre was added to the New Jersey Register of Historical Places, as well as the National Register of Historical Places.

A few years later, a campaign was kicked-off to raise funds for the Strand Theater's restoration, but actual restoration of the theatre did not begin until 1992. Within a year, the Strand Theater reopened as a performing arts center, looking very much like it did when it opened seventy years before.

Story has it that some of the "Old Hoofers" who had once graced the Strand's stage may still be hoofing it and that some of the deceased performers who had become famous still visit from time to time.

Don't Call Us: We'll Call You!

From the 1930s through 1999, AT&T operated a 'high seas' radiotelephone service that allowed oceangoing ships to make and receive telephone calls over high frequency (short-wave) radio. Three land stations were located on the coasts of the United States, one of which was located on the New Jersey shore in Ocean Gate. Each of the stations had a large field of antennas tuned to various frequencies across the short-wave band to accommodate changing radio conditions. The service was finally discontinued, which had largely been rendered obsolete by the advent of satellite telephones, on November 9, 1999.

Radiotelephone antennas.

Wideband wire 'inverted cones' were among the antenna designs used at both the transmitter and receiver sites and the one, decaying after more than ten years of neglect, is located at the ruins of the WOO transmitter site in the marshlands of Ocean Gate. The locals living near this abandoned site have many stories to tell: On moonlit nights, this giant spider web-like antenna seems to make strange sounds as if communicating with something strange. Those who venture here claim that the small brick building will absorb anyone who enters its portals and leave as quickly as possible.

Are these stories only embedded in the minds of those who venture there? You may find out for yourself…should you dare to pay a visit here on some quiet moonlit night.

Giant spiderweb antenna.

Mysterious Giant Fireball Seen off Jersey Shore

What was the strange fire falling from the sky observed over the ocean off the Jersey Shore? As told by the locals, many witnesses were reported to have seen lights falling from the sky ten miles off Normandy Beach, New Jersey, early in September 2007. This mysterious event was also described as a "giant fireball" exploding over the ocean. However, a search team sent by the Coast Guard along with New Jersey State Police found nothing unusual in the area.

At least fifteen witnesses were alleged to have seen this strange event and described the same object falling into the ocean. Who were these witnesses? Who interviewed them? Could the mysterious object be the Aurigid meteor shower producing green/blue lights? This rather rare astronomical event was in fact expected to be seen on September 1, 2007, and seems to emanate from the constellation Auriga. Astronomers say the source of the shower is Comet Kiess (C/1911 N1), a mysterious 'long-period comet' that has visited the inner solar system only twice in the past 2,000 years, but was this the case that the locals were speaking of? Well, as some stories go, they contain half-truths combined with wishful thinking and what would some folklore be without them!

The Father of Our Country and the Delaware

The Delaware River emanates from the Delaware Bay at the southernmost point in New Jersey, near its western shoreline. Sunny beaches dot this coastal area and reaching about one-quarter up the western side of the Garden State.

What is the folklore story of George Washington crossing the Delaware? Did he throw a silver coin across the river?

Let's not mix up two Washington legends. As history is witness, he definitely did cross the Delaware to attack the Hessians in Trenton, New Jersey, during the Revolutionary War. The other story, which is probably not true, is that he once threw a silver dollar across the Potomac River. While we are at it, he also did not chop down a cherry tree and later prove his honesty by saying "I cannot tell a lie."

By the way, like the mythical silver dollar, Mount Vernon did not exist at that time either!

Long Beach Island's Iggity Ag

As a gentle breeze and majestic setting sun sweeps night over the Victorian rooftops in Beach Haven, some locals tell the tale of a shore resident, an old widow, who lived alone in a ramshackle old home. Each day, she would walk along the boulevard in a heavy woolen coat, regardless of temperature, never uttering a word.

The sight was an odd one for visitors and children would follow her around with teasing remarks. They christened her "Iggity Ag" and would mockingly shout her name. About twenty years ago, she passed away, but many people have reported seeing the spectral figure of an old woman, in a heavy overcoat, pacing the sidewalks and street corners. The sound of laughing children accompanies the experiences, a reminder of the harassing hooligans who tormented Iggity Ag.

The Sea Caves

As the locals tell it, Jersey Shore has many sea caves all around its coastline with a few strange tales connected to them. One cannot imagine that if you were to venture into one and never come out, where would you go and what strange situations might occur? Well, I for one do not want to find out, but in some of the known areas tales emerge of individuals simply disappearing, never returning! Claims of some who have come out tell of having a feeling that should they have continued to travel into the deeper depths of the cave they would be sucked in, like a vacuum…the feeling of an endless tunnel to the center of the earth! This type of folklore is what movies are made of and, if the locals are right, would you like to experience this for yourself?

Legend of the Little People of New Jersey

Throughout the world for millennia, stories are passed down of various types of small humanoids and Native American folklore is no exception. Lenni Lenape folklore tells of a race of diminutive beings that dwelt in the forests, which they called the *Wematekan'is*. Typical of the legends of these little people found throughout cultures worldwide, the Wematekan'is were said to be shy and wary of humans. When the Wematekan'is would occasionally interact with the Lenape people, they often played mischievous pranks on the unsuspecting 'Big Folk.'

By the Sea! By the Sea!

You may imagine that Seaside Park is precisely equal to any other municipality in the United States of America, but the phantom tales told by the local residents are enough to make anyone reassess their thoughts a bit. Some folks who live here say these reports are not true, but there truly are unusual things happening here in Seaside Park during the moonlight hours.

One such story is that of a woman, pale looking and faint of figure, you may encounter in search of her husband, who went to war and never returned, simply strolling along on the beach late at night. If you wish, you may approach her, but do not be surprised if she ignores you and keeps on walking, always with the sad expression on her face and her eyes trained toward the sea. As she reaches a certain point on the beach, believed by the locals to be the spot where she had first met her husband, she lingers for a moment and then seems to vanish into the evening's sea air.

The Lighthouse that Refuses to Die

The strong tides were responsible for many shipwrecks along the length of Long Beach Island. As a result, a lighthouse was built on the northern end of the Island. Barnegat Lighthouse is still standing and is open to the public during the summer. The lighthouse was automated in 1927, but would only remain in service another seventeen years. After World War II, the lighthouse was decommissioned and given to the state of New Jersey.

Now, you may not give second thoughts to this if it were not for, what seems to be, the mysterious blinking of the lighthouse light on stormy nights when the sea is rough and the howling wind's echoing laughter resounds as if it were riding on the waves beating against the rocks; as some of the local inhabitants tell it.

Richard's Own Ghost Train to Nowhere!

I thought it would be fitting to conclude this chapter with a little story of my own.

Growing up in Newark, New Jersey, as a young lad, I can recall that when the hot days of summer became a reality, some members of my father's side of our family would take a week's rental at a lonely stretch of beach known then as 'Charlie's Beach'. Ironically, my father's nickname was Charlie. I remember that this was in the summer of 1945 because I recall reports of the war in Europe nearing its end. If my recollection serves me correctly, this particular Charlie's Beach was located at or near Keyport, New Jersey; however, I am not certain if this beach is still in existence today. Now, my dad would go there for an overnight on one of the weekends that the family was there and would take me along. My mother always stayed at home, as she did not care that much for ocean bathing.

Usually, we would arrive there early evening on a Friday and return home on Sunday. Since we did not go for a dip in the ocean in the evening, I would be on my own to amuse myself while my father sat and chatted with family members. A short distance from the bungalow was a railroad track and I would place a coin on one of the tracks at the sound of a train whistle; the coin would be flattened, usually to double its original size.

On one of these occasions as storm clouds were beginning to form and thunder could be heard, the sky beginning to darken, I heard the sound of a train whistle, quickly putting my coin on the track and waited, knowing that my father would be calling me to come in soon. Now, this may sound a bit strange, as it did to me at the time, but I could hear the sound of the train passing and could feel the breeze, but no train was visible. This was not my imagination as the strange part of all this was that my coin had been flattened by this "ghost" train to nowhere!

It was not until many years later I discovered that a long-time railroad engineer who's run that was had died suddenly during that same summer. Was he still making his run and was I fortunate to have been there at the time?

NOTE: I wish to emphasize that it is not a good practice to permit children to play near railroad tracks.

Understanding Spirits and What NJGO Does

Every location does not have a history or at least the type of history that makes us curious. An area can and may have a connection, so much so that a particular event, whether it is tragic or not can leave an "imprint", which enables us to experience something.

Animals seem to have a heightened sixth-sense and it is important to note that perhaps your pet may be aware of something before you are aware. It is also important to keep a log or jot down something that you may have witnessed that cannot be explained, something unusual and we listen to your claims of activity and experiences.

Spirits can interact with the living but, always keep foremost in your mind they were at one time alive as you are today and are entitled to have the same respect given to them as you would have others give to you. Some will continue to cross over and others may wish to remain earthbound. Spirits that crossover may travel back and forth between both worlds; they can warn us, send us a message, or engage in any number of activities. Why we can see them is not completely known. The ones that have not crossed over, most often, have not realized that they are no longer among the living simply because they cannot accept not being so. You may see spirits out of the corner of your eye, feel them, and even smell them at times. They may also interact in many ways to let you know that they are still around through sounds, movement of objects, etc.

Ghosts are an "imprint" left, their energy is left-over and we are surrounded by energy, that under certain atmospheric conditions is the reason as to why we can see them. Many times their actions may seem real and deliberate to us, but are really nothing more than repetitious and residual. They are not aware of us simply because this is like watching a scene that had once taken place but one that cannot be interacted with by either those in it or by yourself watching it. These usually take place unexpectedly; you may simply turn a corner to experience this phenomenon.

Spirits do not show up on command; however, we can try and establish contact with them, but there are never any guarantees. That is why we continue to do research and continue attempting to capture their images on film, video or to hear them on audio by having an understanding of physics and thermodynamics.

By using various, similar types of equipment, we also try to document our findings in order to support any evidence we may gather. This is a common goal among all paranormal investigators.

Ask and thou shalt (may) receive is a good mantra that should be considered and you may pleasantly be surprised with your results.

A Double-Edged Sword: TV vs. Paranormal Investigating

As founder and lead investigator of a paranormal group, I feel it is important that certain aspects of paranormal investigating have some light shed upon them. In recent years, the field of "ghost hunting," although a commonly referred to term but one that I do not prefer to use, has exploded with television showcasing and presenting paranormal investigating in the entertainment arena. They lend themselves to many inaccuracies and fallacies. Fortunately, most reputable groups are skilled enough to be able to overcome this and garner much more in the way of positive evidence, lending more substance in preserving the future of the paranormal field.

In paranormal investigating, we do use what true science may consider as pseudo-scientific equipment; however, we are not scientists and, therefore, what we accomplish is not recognized in the scientific field as "proof positive" that spirits, "ghosts," or residual hauntings exist. We do have, with the equipment that we use, an understanding of basic physics, the laws of thermodynamics, and the theories as to how and why we obtain the results that we do when investigating.

We are following in the shadows of many great inventors, scientists, and researchers and have modified certain equipment to better suit our requirements. To those individuals we will forever be indebted. My philosophy and experience in leading a group that has barely scratched the paranormal surface, being in this field for a little over eight years, is that the simplest of equipment is all one needs and that knowledge and understanding is a more important factor. The challenge is to make the equipment work for you and you will find that better results will follow.

Paranormal investigating, via the entertainment media has created a double-edge sword. While paranormal investigating is exciting and most often rewarding, because there are dozens of television shows showcasing ghosts and ghost hunting, there are many more groups cropping up and it has become increasingly popular, but for all the wrong reasons. I have noticed that quite a few of the television off-shoot groups seem to fizzle out in a very short time, as they discover that every house is not haunted.

What has become most distressing is that since the "entertainment ghost hunting" shows have come into being, whether good or poorly orchestrated, have set the scene and many historical locations have succumbed to the "ghost of greed", asking entrance fees to investigate and placing impossible insurance demands on groups. Unfortunately, time and society have forgotten about many historically significant places however, on the other edge of the sword, many reputable paranormal groups have a genuine respect for history and do not want to forget about those places.

Yes, the television shows have brought attention to and, undoubtedly, business for these incredible places in history, but at what price to paranormal investigating?

Chapter 27

Team Spirit

When I founded New Jersey Ghost Organization, it was with the intention, as well as most newly founded paranormal groups, to do what our predecessors did and are still doing — follow well-established protocols and procedures and change them, if only for the better. By maintaining these practices, I call them "Rules to Live By," each member is a responsible part of this unification of the entire group. Each and every member must be on the same page. You don't want people who continually test the rules. A group effort is a win for everyone. You want people in your group that have the same level of integrity to keep the group moving forward, the same high level of honesty and people that you can depend on to get the job done, and done well whether there is a couple of people in your group or several. You also need to set the example of a show of respect and expect the same in return. If you are a new group just beginning, in which we also feel new to the paranormal community, even though we've been around for several years, these are things that you are continually learning and improving upon. Learning about equipment, understanding its uses and how it relates to or how we can adapt it to make it useful to what we do. Is there something we can improve upon without getting too technical? Researching something new you've seen or heard about, surfing the Internet to see how the paranormal community is growing. It never hurts to experiment either. You don't know until you try.

As the saying goes, there is no 'I' in the word team. There is so much information and examples of evidence and groups out there that if you study it, you really cannot go wrong. As time goes on you will be able to tell the more informative from that of the lesser and you will come through with flying colors, on the good side of course. What works the best is keeping things simple, keeping the 'Rules to Live By' simple, keeping the workload simple, and keeping the equipment we use simple. It is important to remember that sometimes the knowledge is more important than the fancy equipment. Delegation of responsibility is very important and you need individuals that you can depend on and trust. So, by keeping things simple is usually what works the best and always keeping in mind that being open to suggestions is a vital part of the road to success. One of your team members just may have a better solution or better way of accomplishing a specific goal. What you want to avoid is making people a part of your team who seem to not be dependable, or who create distractions or drama. This brings the group down and can stall progress.

You want to put forth the best possible, documented evidence that you can. You will accomplish that by learning, growing, and putting in an honest days' or nights' work. There is so much information and examples of evidence and groups out there you really cannot go wrong. As time goes on you'll be able to tell the good from the bad; you want to come through with flying colors.

Experience is the Best Teacher

When you work with knowledgeable individuals, it gives you the type of edge you need when going over potentially extraordinary evidence. A trained photographer can help debunk a photo as well as spot something that possibly the average ghost hunter may miss. During an investigation, we typically photograph in the dark and a good portion of the time spent taking photographs is basically random shots. Among the many photographs are those of specific areas where there have been reports of unusual activity. Generally, these would be areas that you would concentrate on carefully as opposed to some of the lesser-reported activity. By this we mean you are noticing your surroundings for potential interference simply because you are spending a greater amount of time in these areas.

When doing a walk-through at the beginning of an investigation, you are not only looking for unsafe areas and obstacles — we always do the initial walkthrough with the lights on and some psychics prefer doing their initial "impressions" walk with the lights on — but you, the investigator, are also looking and photographing each area 360 degrees. By doing so, you can easily refer back to those photos when in doubt during examination of potential evidence. This is the first part of a walk-through and the second part would be taking initial temperature readings to identify electromagnetic fields that may be present.

When photographing in the dark, it does not preclude that your flash may pick up a reflection in a specific area, one resembling or giving the appearance of something paranormal, this potential is always present and is a big factor in misinterpreting evidence. However, you can definitely go back to your walkthrough 360-degree photos and see exactly what could have caused something that seems of a paranormal nature that was captured in your photo.

When our group first started investigating, we visited a local cemetery. In one of the photos, off in the distance, there appeared to be a "ghostly figure," but because we photographed the cemetery 360 degrees while it was still daylight, we were able to confirm that this was not a "ghostly figure" — it was merely an individual's headstone that happened to be Jewish and Jewish tradition is to have the headstone covered with a white cloth until such anniversary the cloth is removed. Likely what occurred was the white cloth became a reflective surface and even though it was dark out, the moonlight may have served as just enough light, just enough of an angle, to catch and photograph it that way.

We investigated a church and its adjoining cemetery early on after forming our group. When we looked over our photos, we noticed this bright green color in a couple of the church's windows. It reminds you of the green-goop in the movie *Ghostbusters*. Actually it was the reflection of very tall trees with their green, full leaves hiding a light pole. Distorted, but that was it. To be absolutely positive, and because this church was close by, we double backed and checked the timing on the light against the time the photographs were taken. Sure enough this was the reason, which went unnoticed on our first visit. The light apparently was solar powered. Those photos were tossed. Interesting, but tossed.

On investigating outdoors, it is a given that many things can and will go wrong. Indoor investigations are a little more complicated. An example of that would be the faux-pas at the Burlington County Prison mentioned in an earlier chapter. When putting forth genuine evidence, it's important not to take your photos for granted or that they are the truth until close examination. It's also important when people come up to you and show you their own photographs taken in their homes or on vacation, not to take them too seriously. After all, you weren't there when they were taken. You need to investigate their claims much further and see if they have something to back that up with. The average person may not see things the same way you do.

Eyes Wide Open

Why do unusual anomalies show up in photographs? There are simple explanations for most; however, there may not be any for others. Typically on investigations we photograph with the lights out, but this is really not necessarily a factor and a considerable number of the photographs that are taken are considered basically random shots. Our belief, and the belief of many, is that if a spirit wishes to allow their image to be reproduced on either film or by digital electronics they will. The many photographs of specific areas having reports of activity are areas you would concentrate on making simple to examine when viewing the results. By this we mean you are noticing your surroundings for potential interference a little more carefully because you are spending a larger amount of time in those specific areas. The role that the investigator takes on can help in a different way.

It is actually a two-part situation on walk-throughs: Taking photographs is the first and the second would naturally be in making notations of the initial temperatures and identifying electromagnetic fields within the various areas of the location. Whether you are photographing with the lights on or off, it doesn't necessarily mean because you are not using a flash, that you are not going to pick up a reflection somewhere in a specific area. The potential is always there, but you can definitely go back to your walk-through 360-degree photos and see exactly what could have caused something that seems to be paranormal in nature appearing in your photo.

Chapter 28

Not Alone

We are convinced that we definitely do not walk alone. Psychics have told both Richard and I on numerous occasions that there is someone always with us. These psychics have basically told us the same things for us to come to the same conclusions that these pieces of information are true. As an example, my dad always has a woman beside him, attached to him. Through information relayed by psychics, and very specific things, we had determined the spirit was that of his mother, my grandmother.

In my case, I have been told things on two levels. The first I have been told is there is a young girl attached to me, she is very interested in the type of work I am doing, meaning work in the paranormal field. Now this I was acutely aware of as it came to me in the form of a dream.

This story begins with a dream where I was walking along with, who I believe was this young girl, long before any psychic informed me of this. It was a paved road, near where my family and I once lived. I had just left the apartment and for whatever reason was barefoot and she began walking along with me on my left side. I would have estimated her to be in her early teens at best. I had a piece of cake on a small plate in my hand. The young girl and I were having a conversation about someone who was coming home from the hospital and I asked the girl to please bring this piece of cake to this "someone." We walked a short distance along the road and I had said to her that I could not go any farther and thanked her. This was the end of the dream, at least for now.

I have never had this dream again and the reason why is that this someone I referred to earlier was my husband's best man when we were married. Many years later our best man committed suicide. The time that I had this dream coincided with the anniversary of our best man's death, which I was not even thinking about. I was curious as to why I had this dream this year and not all of the other years that had passed? This year would be special; ten months later would be my husband's and my twenty-fifth wedding anniversary. Our best man did not want to be forgotten. This was his way of reminding us, through this young girl in my dream. I could not go with her, hence my having bare feet and at that point in time I was not able to be on the "other side." The piece of cake was the symbol of an anniversary or celebration. An interesting thing I found out later from my husband was that this particular year he did not visit our best man's grave, which he had done every year since his passing. Other things had occupied his mind and he had simply forgotten.

What we decided to do the day after our twenty-fifth wedding anniversary was pay our best man's gravesite a visit. My husband and I left two roses on his grave to let him know that we had not forgotten about him, which we never did before, and in a way it was like having him celebrate our anniversary with us.

I have since been informed that this same young girl seems to be with me a great deal of the time. I would imagine that she is some sort of angel, almost like a guardian angel. I have never seen her face and most details about her I cannot recall.

On another level, psychics have told me that I am here for a greater purpose, that I had volunteered for this reincarnation and that I will not be finished until God has returned. However, I don't think I will live long enough to see the end of the world. There is something I have to do for God. Seems crazy, right? I simply will not really know until it happens. With that, I have been told that there is an "entire team" from the "other side" watching and guiding me, a woman with white hair leading them. Apparently, I seem, in their estimation, a handful or possibly not? It would seem that there are things that have yet to be accomplished and I have been chosen to help accomplish this.

As I lay down one night awaiting sleep, I suddenly became very comfortable and began to drift off. In my mind's eye this woman's face appeared to come up to mine, seeming to swoop in from the left, and then back to the left again. From the expression on her face I could tell she was a large woman of sorts. Her hair pulled back tightly, and having a slight stern look on her face. It made me feel like I had done something wrong. The next day I quickly thought about what I had done, much less anything wrong, but could not think of anything.

I guess you can relate this directly to being a paranormal investigator. What we, most investigators are doing to move the paranormal field forward is a huge task. Getting the evidence and supporting it is very important. You have to work extremely hard, do your homework and then work even harder especially considering the many new groups popping up all over the country and immediately referring to themselves as, having absolutely no prior experience, "paranormal investigative groups." Most often, they seem to put any photo they take up on the Internet and call it evidence. They watch all the paranormal programs on television and believe that they can go out there and do it as well. Well, you can, but you also need to have a true understanding of what you are doing. Some do not have a clue, and this is serious business not a game!

On the other hand, it is not necessary to possess a great deal of experience or a defining dream to understand or realize that you are on your way to putting successful evidence out into the paranormal community. Sometimes it is the smallest piece of evidence that will convince you that you are on the right track.

For example, our group was called upon to do an investigation a couple of years ago at a private home. We set up all of our equipment, and decided to secure the premises, leaving the cameras run for awhile and along with the homeowner went for a short a walk, as the historic Gabriel-Davies Tavern was just a couple of blocks away and we had never been there before. This tavern was of the revolutionary era and we were curious to see if we could catch a glimpse of what or who may still be lingering there, knowing it was closed to the public.

While we were walking, and just stepping onto the roadway leading to the tavern, the psychic that was with us (not knowing this at the time) felt and saw the spirit of a woman in revolutionary period clothing walking along the roadway with us only several yards away and going in the same direction as we were and the psychic immediately snapped a photo with hopes of capturing the image. At the same time, I had also felt as if something was with us, not being psychic and not knowing what the psychic had seen and felt.

When we viewed the photos, in the one that the psychic had taken there was an orb in the exact spot where the psychic had seen and felt the spirit.

I am convinced that we definitely do not walk alone!

Chapter 29

Give Me Shelter

The tales that overshadow this time capsule has found their way as far southeast as the New Jersey shore and Jerseyans flock there to see if the stories they have been hearing are more than just that or are they simply folklore that has been a bit exaggerated?

The investigation by NJGO was an opportunity of a lifetime, to walk in the footsteps of greatness, some of our founding fathers and signers of the Declaration of Independence, not one, but ten and a first lady. It's such a different feeling from other investigations whenever we investigate a historical building. It's history, in your face! You always feel like you've stepped back in time and wondered what it was like to live during what seems like such both exciting and trying times. The American Revolution, the making and the beginning of our country, what would become the United States of America and free from British rule. It also makes you think about the hardships these people faced and what life was like over 250 years ago. However, the Sun Inn in Bethlehem, Pennsylvania was host to not only the townspeople and people traveling through the area, but hosted a very impressive list of people whose names we are very familiar with; John Adams, Samuel Adams, John Hancock, General George Washington and Martha Washington to name some.

A Spirited Vacancy

A group of Moravian Missionaries settled in Bethlehem in the year 1741. These particular groups of people were also skilled craftspeople. In less than ten years they had a thriving economy, which included their own blacksmith shop, pottery building and tannery, including developing a spring water system for the town. People came from as far as Philadelphia just to do business with them. Since folks traveled so far the missionaries built the Sun Inn in 1758 and opened for business in 1760. The Inn, a Germanic stone building stood tall for approximately two hundred years until falling into disrepair. We heard an account of some of the paranormal activity that takes place on a regular basis, as well as the Inn twice was the site of the Continental Hospital specifically during the battle at Brandywine in 1777.

The Investigation

We chose the "Gast-Stube" Room (German word for gathering place) to convene to begin our investigation. Very fitting. We also began our investigation in this room. With mobile video cameras in two places to cover the room, right from the very beginning we kept seeing shadows in the main doorway of this room. Something or someone was in the lobby. The KII meter (electromagnetic field detector) would also set off. Whatever it was or whoever even came so far as a foot or so into the room.

We spent time in the many rooms doing EVP sessions, videotaping, and photographing throughout the night. However, in one of the Inn's several suites gave off a different type of atmosphere. The Martha Washington Suite felt like a lot of activity went on in there, a hurried feeling, and anxiousness. The Inn confirmed that when undergoing renovations they discovered behind the walls the original shutters, intact, which happen to be on the inside, not the outside of the building. If they should be under attack, they could easily close the shutters to avoid detection. You had the feeling of children being in this suite and being told to keep quiet as not to bother other guests staying at the Inn. This room had two bedrooms and one outer room. Each of the two bedrooms had completely different feelings. When one of our team was photographing, upon examination of these photos, the second of the three photos shows what appears to be a woman's head in the lower corner, perhaps one of the Inn's housekeepers?

We did a group EVP session up on the third floor in one of the huge dining rooms. We asked some questions along with our psychic present. She conveyed to us from a spirit about the flower gardens in the back are gone, all of which was confirmed by the Inn. On the voice recorder we picked up "flower garden missing." Throughout this EVP session we through our psychic had gotten things like "Beginning of Peace Making" and "Didn't want the Capital here." The Inn confirmed all of which.

After leaving the Inn and returning home to Jersey, upon review of all possible evidence, another photo revealed two faces in a window between floors on the staircases that another one of our team took. These images appeared not to be in clothing from our time period.

Analysis

It is almost as if the spirits want you to see them on their terms sometimes and that they want you to know that there is still "life" in these old buildings. Nothing seemed bad or malevolent, nothing to be feared. Active spirits realize and recognize when something has changed from what used to be. It also seems as though they are curious, and at times interested in what we as investigators are doing. To an investigator it's comforting to know that perhaps we do indeed coexist from one world to another, after hundreds of years passing. From our perspective it is nice to hear their voices and catch glimpses of them. Sometimes it is almost as if we've traveled back in history.

Sun Inn face photo.
Courtesy of Cathy Sansevere.

Chapter 30

Outside of the Box

We decided to take up the kind offer of another New Jersey paranormal group and do a joint investigation. We in turn extended the offer to another paranormal group in the town in which I live. Both of these groups have the same standard of protocols and the same level of integrity as our group does, so there was absolutely no hesitation on anyone's part not to do this. Actually, we all looked forward to take a road trip to upstate New York.

This was not an average investigation for us. At first I thought about everything that could go wrong: too many people, a lot of expensive equipment, and the possibility of compromised evidence. So we tried to rationalize all of those thoughts and try and come up with ways to avert a possible investigative disaster. This weighed on my mind in the weeks before the trip until we reached our destination.

The Spirits Are "Inn"

"The Spirits Are Inn" is what the sign reads over the front door of the Shanley Hotel. The Shanley is located in Napanoch, New York, in Hudson Valley near the Shawanugunk Mountains. This is not your average place. It is an eight thousand square foot Victorian era hotel set in its very own ghost town of sorts. There is not much to do in the town. Picture a town similar to the old TV show Mayberry. Any business in the area has long closed before the sunsets. The owners are a husband and wife that are as nice as can be, hardworking and are excited to tell you the hotel's history.

The original hotel was built in 1845 boasting to be a popular summer vacation destination, which included the area's finest of foods until in 1895 when the hotel burned to its foundation. Later in the same year the Shanley was rebuilt. Over the years even to this day, ownership has changed hands many, many times. The most notable owner was a man named James Shanley from New York City; he purchased the hotel in 1906. Four years later he married and thus began many years of being socialites entertaining people such as a President and Mrs. Franklin Roosevelt. Mr. Shanley passed away in 1937 and in 1944 Mrs. Shanley sold the hotel and moved back to New York City.

Along with the glamour and glitz also came many tragedies in and around the Shanley Hotel. Numerous children died and there were childbirth deaths, accidental drowning, missing persons, suicides and murders, as well as bootlegging, prostitution, and arrests. The Shanley is furnished in Victorian style in most of the thirty-five rooms, but a hotel would not be complete without what was once a private gentleman's club quarters, a brothel, a tunnel, which was used during the Underground Railroad era and a hidden room, used to hide during the prohibition era. The owners will tell you they have reports of every kind of paranormal activity you can imagine, so of course we couldn't wait to begin investigating.

The Investigation

It was just the beginning of what promised to be a long and hot summer, but we made it — all three paranormal groups gathered on the long porch of the Shanley Hotel just before the sun was about to set. Toting both equipment and luggage we were greeted by Sal and Cindy. It wasn't long before we ascended to the upper floor to decide what rooms we would occupy for the night. Afterwards some of us took a short walk through the woods to a nearby restaurant for a quick bite to eat before beginning the investigation, while some stayed behind to linger on the front porch for some conversation. When we returned inside, we began an official tour of the hotel, heard the reports of "paranormal" experiences, heard a little of the history of the hotel and began to set up our equipment. We actually started photographing since we arrived, and our group's psychic was beginning to get a feel for the place. An experience I had almost immediately was the whisper of a man's voice directly in my ear, I could feel the vibration, but I could not distinguish what was said. It's later on in the evening and we begin to set up, running cables for the IR cameras, tossing the cables down through the main staircases and securing them, some investigators brought new pieces of equipment to experiment with and after everything and everyone settled in we began to pair off to do some EVP sessions, photograph and let the IR cameras run. Everyone took his or her time. It seemed like a very odd and relaxing time, not your typical investigation. I wouldn't exactly call it a vacation. Everyone was working on something. We were the only people in the hotel.

One of the more stand out personal experiences two of our group's members had was in what the paranormal community calls dead time. It is the time after midnight but before the morning light, specifically 3 a.m. where it would appear the veil is the thinnest and the easiest to see and experience actual paranormal activity. Two of our members were sitting in the main room of the hotel. My recollection was this occurred around 4 a.m. All of our other members, as well as the other two groups had gone to sleep. Beyond this main room is a bathroom, the gentleman's club quarters in which we had three of our members sleeping in and you had stairs going up to the brothel. The member that was sleeping in the brothel couldn't sleep and joined Richard down in the main room. This area of the hotel I don't believe is connected to the main part of the hotel, otherwise you would be on the hotel's second floor. From the outside it appears this section is a Dutch style structure. All of a sudden both members heard very loud and quick footsteps on the stairs leading to the brothel and both ran over to the stairs and began photographing. Going quickly up the stairs to the Brothel still photographing however, there was absolutely nothing or no one there. Should there have been a person on the staircase it would have been easy to see someone entering or exiting that stairway. They knew that at the time no one was occupying the brothel. We knew where all of the investigators were sleeping. An unknown. Nothing appeared in their photos as well. This is just another example of many occurrences both on this investigation and other investigations we encounter.

In the brothel earlier that evening another team member's hair on her arm was standing straight up and felt that eerie coldness when in the presence of a spirit with two team members witnessing this experience. A single orb was captured on a couple of occasions exactly in that area. An orb is a circular anomalous sphere, self-luminous very concentrated form of energy associated with spirit presence. Orbs are always up for debate whether they are an actual spirit attempting to manifest into something more significant or it is a spirit gathering energy. From time to time we've actually captured on camera images in which you can distinguish male or female inside these bright white balls of energy.

If one of our psychics comes along with us on an investigation, they always bring their camera. Who better than to have take photos when they can see spirits, right? While she was walking around taking photos she happened to take a photo of the main staircase. At one point or another during our stay most of us photographed this staircase. The difference was we didn't get anything unusual in those particular photos when we all got together to review evidence, except for our psychic. The staircase was wooden but had carpeting going up the middle. On the wooden part of the stairs on several of the steps you can see faces, all different faces, and the image of a cat's face. Our psychic was the only one to capture this.

Another one of our members took a photo of the outside of the hotel and one of her photos revealed what looked like a cat lying in one of the third floor windows. We were familiar with what was up on that floor and there was nothing on the window ledge to make you think you could be mistaken. Now the owners will tell you their cat passed away about the year before.

Shanley hallway photo.

Is it possible to capture this? It's very possible. At one point I had gone up to the third floor alone, I wanted to check one of our IR video cameras. I always have another member monitor the quad in a situation of going in an area alone. All three groups were monitoring our respective quads from the hotel's main room. Well, the third floor is exactly like the second floor as far as the building's design; only the third floor is not lavishly decorated. As a matter of fact, it's just the opposite — unfinished, unpainted, and ongoing construction. I get up to the third floor and, after checking the IR camera, I decided to walk the hallway and take a look in each of the rooms. I had taken photos of this floor much earlier in the evening, but you know how you get that feeling of being drawn to an area.

So I wanted to re-photograph each room. When I got up there my camera started giving me trouble, on again, off again so I went down to the main floor to get fresh batteries. The same thing occurred with my flashlight. It can not only be frustrating, but annoying when you know you just changed the batteries no more than the hour before and didn't need to have either one on constantly. This can happen when there is spirit presence; they can draw on any electronic equipment you may be using. Now I continue back up to the third floor to continue photographing. I get to the start of the long hallway and now I am almost regretting coming up alone, because I get the feeling I am not alone. I got about halfway down and decided to go no further, but took a photo from where I stood. After we returned home from our trip to the Shanley and went over the evidence, I couldn't believe I could get so lucky.

The next morning, as everyone was getting up, we chatted and had breakfast, compliments of Sal and Cindy. It was such a beautiful day and some gathered on the front porch, some inside the main room to eat, not

Shanley hallway close-up.

really feeling like breaking down all of the equipment. But it was a job that had to get done. The Hotel definitely takes on a different feel at night. Most of us had done some EVP sessions with our roomies in our rooms the night before, and we felt we had covered just about everything we wanted to cover and eventually we were eager to get back home and look at the evidence. It was just such a different departure from the investigations we were accustomed to. Sure we've been in "haunted," much larger, older structures before, even a few prisons so chilling enough to drain all of your blood to your feet, but this one was just different. We've done investigations with other paranormal groups before on occasion, so that wasn't it. It's like going out to Trick or Treat and coming home with a bag load of candy. You never know what you're going to get. It doesn't sound very professional, but nonetheless, a good analogy. I was also a little nervous working with a dozen investigators, triple the equipment, but was hoping we would get some evidence. Did we? Absolutely.

The Analysis

We all had the chance to look over evidence, and later on in the days that followed had the opportunity to arrange with the other two groups to get together once again and discuss and exchange information. Our group had gotten some very compelling photographs while the other two groups had some great EVPs. We could conclude that there are both residual ghosts and active spirits here based on our evidence. In one instance, one of the EVPs said, "Lisa, Help." Lisa is one of our team members. What are the chances that a voice recorded mentions her name on the very same visit we are there? Unfortunately, we can't help them unless they make themselves known. As far as the footsteps on the stairs leading to the Brothel, it was a heads up for our two members who heard the footsteps, were they too late?

It seems as though some photographic evidence we got was with the help of our psychic's awareness. Many of the team photographed that main staircase with no results. The psychic is drawn to specific areas and she was the only one who photographed those faces on the stairs. It's our opinion that at this particular location luck played a huge part that you had to be at the right place at the right time, as if you had to catch these spirits and ghosts off guard. Maybe some of us whose sixth sense isn't as keen as a psychic's started to kick in. Something heightened my senses not to continue down the one hallway on the third floor. So I took the photo from where I stopped in my tracks. Maybe the battery drains both on my camera and my flashlight sometimes indicating spirit presence should have been the deciding factor. Obviously it was, because I went downstairs to change the batteries. It was only then upon my return to go back up and now take that photo. Maybe any sooner or later that image wouldn't have been captured walking in front of that window. It would seem that timing is everything. There is a reason for everything or so it seems. Pay attention to the warning signs.

A Glossary of Paranormal Terms

The following are some of the more commonly used terms by paranormal investigators.

Ectoplasm: A spectral trail left behind by spirits. In its primary form, it looks like a fog.

EMF (Electromagnetic Field) Detector: An instrument common to paranormal investigators, it is used as an aid in tracking energy sources. It detects fluctuations in electromagnetic fields. A common theory is that spirits disrupt this electromagnetic field when present, thereby giving off a higher reading on this device.

Ghost: A sighting or recording of a past routine or event of an individual. This is energy that rejuvenates or recharges under certain atmospheric conditions, repetitious, intensely emotional for that individual. Think of a murder scene or a battlefield. It will gradually lose energy over time.

Manifestation: Typically a combination of various forms of tangible signs — temperature changes, visual, touch, sound — that can be scientifically supported.

Materialization: The process by which a spirit creates a physical representation of itself in the physical world.

Orbs: Unexplainable circles or balls of white light; it's a very concentrated form of energy associated with a spirit's presence.

Paranormal: Anything out of the normal range of an explanation; an event that defies current scientific knowledge.

Paranormal Investigator: A person who investigates a haunting to find explanations, document, record, and photograph paranormal phenomena using scientific equipment and methods in order to obtain and support accurate calculations, observations, and experiences.

Percipient: An individual involved with or observing a paranormal occurrence. Any repeated appearance of phenomena commonly associated with ghosts, spirits, or poltergeists that tend to be witnessed by more than one person.

Portal: An area in a location where spirits can come and go easily between both worlds; theoretically a doorway of energy.

Psychic/Intuitive: A person who has a heightened, fully developed sixth sense and has the ability to obtain information based on unexplainable intuition, visions, and senses to communicate with a spirit or learn about a haunting.

Spirit: Not to be confused with a "Ghost", this is the actual soul of a person that has passed on as they interact with us. They are observed because of several things: A spirit does not realize they are dead, they have unfinished business, or they have information to tell.

Thermometer: An instrument used to observe temperature changes in any given area. Paranormal investigators use this to observe extreme or rapid temperature drops associated with spirit presence.

Voice Recorders/EVP: Electronic Voice Phenomenon is active spirit voice frequently captured on voice recorders. In the case of a residual haunting their voice is picked up on voice recorders because their voice, actions, death, or all of the above left an imprint in a specific location.

Vortex: The center of spiritual energy; usually an area that is displaying signs of manifestation in a very specific area.

Warp: A location where the known laws of physics do not always apply and space and time may be distorted.

Epilogue

Folklore, history, and the paranormal go hand in hand and should certain theories be believed then haunting may be caused by high emotions, trauma and pain, each leaving scars on buildings and objects. Therefore, it stands to reason that certain circumstances and structures simply lend themselves to such markings. Filled to the brim with refuse and memories, what happens to those places when society no longer has a use for them? They stand empty keeping their secrets until the last and simply providing a home for restless souls for all eternity who wait with the hope that one day someone, anyone, will come inside to glimpse the past and make contact with them. As paranormal investigators, this may be our destiny and those with the psychic gift to free these souls helping them to move on. All of this is the spawning ground for folklore and as some of the stories passing down through the decades, and yes even the centuries, tend to have tiny twists added. Where do folklore tales begin and where do they end is something that only time will determine, with some simply fading into the abyss.

We have only been able crack open the door of what awaits you here in New Jersey from some areas where we have had personal experiences or have heard instances over the years and featuring some of the New Jersey Ghost Organization's major investigations; the remainder will be yours to discover and experience.

It would be remiss should we not stress that some of the locations may be currently off limits to public access and that it would be wise to either check with the owner or in some cases with the authorities before your venture begins. The New Jersey Ghost Organization has made it their practice to get permission whenever possible.

With the addition of the informational chapters we hope that the technical aspects of our experience will enhance your folklore ventures and make it easier for you to understand what may await you and be able to deal with any unusual situation that may arise. Keep in mind that there is no blueprint to folklore and you may uncover many additional stories that you may find fascinating to carry back home with you from your visit to New Jersey's Shore, passing them on to future generations.

To all of our readers, we certainly hope that you enjoyed reading about some of the unusual locations here at the New Jersey Shore and that you have gained an insight into what entails true professionalism in "Ghost Hunting" and we wish you all the best of luck with your quest in following the folklore trails of the New Jersey Shore, you never know where they may lead you, even into the realm of the Paranormal. Former President Franklin D. Roosevelt once profoundly said, "The only thing that you have to fear, is fear itself"

Thank you for joining us in our traveling the folklore roads of the Jersey Shore and happy legend chasing!

Richard and Karen

Index